Say It Right in

BRAZILIAN PORTUGUESE

**Easily Pronounced
Language Systems, Inc.**

Clyde Pete

New York Chicago San Francisco Lisbon London Madrid Mexico City
Milan New Delhi San Juan Seoul Singapore Sydney Toronto

The McGraw·Hill Companies

Library of Congress Cataloging-in-Publication Data

Say it right in Brazilian Portuguese : the easy way to correct pronunciation! /
   by Easily Pronounced Language Systems.
       p.   cm. — (Say it right)
      Includes bibliographical references and index.
      ISBN 0-07-149230-5 (alk. paper)
      1. Portuguese language—Pronunciation.   2. Portuguese language—
Provincialisms—Brazil.   I. Easily Pronounced Language Systems.   II. Series.

   PC5079.S29   2007
   469.7'98—dc22   2007032036

1 2 2 4 5 6 7 8 9 10 11 12 13 14 15 16 17 18 19 20   LBM/LBM   0 9 8

ISBN 978-0-07-149230-0
MHID   0-07-149230-5

McGraw-Hill books are available at special quantity discounts to use as
premiums and sales promotions or for use in corporate training programs.
To contact a representative, please visit the Contact Us pages at
www.mhprofessional.com.

Also available: *Say It Right in Arabic* • *Say It Right in French* • *Say It Right in German*
• *Say It Right in Italian* • *Say It Right in Japanese* • *Say It Right in Korean* • *Say It
Right in Russian* • *Say It Right in Spanish* • *Dígalo correctamente en inglés [Say It
Right in English]*

Author: Clyde Peters
Illustrations: Luc Nisset
President, EPLS Corporation: Betty Chapman
Senior Series Editor: Priscilla Leal Bailey
Brazilian Portuguese Language Consultant: Renee Gascon

This book is printed on acid-free paper.

CONTENTS

INTRODUCTION

The SAY IT RIGHT FOREIGN LANGUAGE PHRASE BOOK SERIES has been developed with the conviction that learning to speak a foreign language should be fun and easy!

All SAY IT RIGHT phrase books feature the EPLS Vowel Symbol System, a revolutionary phonetic system that stresses consistency, clarity, and above all, simplicity!

Since this unique phonetic system is used in all SAY IT RIGHT phrase books, you only have to learn the VOWEL SYMBOL SYSTEM ONCE!

The SAY IT RIGHT series uses the easiest phrases possible for English speakers to pronounce and is designed to reflect how foreign languages are used by native speakers.

You will be amazed at how confidence in your pronunciation leads to an eagerness to talk to other people in their own language.

Whether you want to learn a new language for travel, education, business, study, or personal enrichment, SAY IT RIGHT phrase books offer a simple and effective method of pronunciation and communication.

PRONUNCIATION GUIDE

Most English speakers are familiar with the Portuguese word **Rio**. This is how the correct. pronunciation is.represented in the EPLS Vowel Symbol System.

All Portuguese vowel sounds are assigned a specific non-changing symbol. When these symbols are used in conjunction with consonants and read normally, pronunciation of even the most difficult foreign word becomes incredibly EASY!

On the following page are all the EPLS Vowel Symbols used in this book. They are EASY to LEARN since their sounds are familiar. Beneath each symbol are three English words which contain the sound of the symbol.

Practice pronouncing the words under each symbol until you mentally associate the correct vowel sound with the correct symbol. Most symbols are pronounced the way they look!

THE SAME BASIC SYMBOLS ARE USED IN ALL SAY IT RIGHT PHRASE BOOKS!

EPLS VOWEL SYMBOL SYSTEM

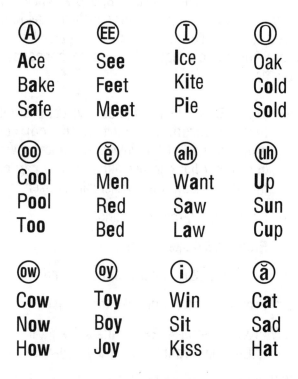

Ⓐ	**ⒺⒺ**	**Ⓘ**	**Ⓞ**
Ace	See	Ice	Oak
Bake	Feet	Kite	Cold
Safe	Meet	Pie	Sold
ⓄⓄ	**ⓔ**	**ⓐⓗ**	**ⓤⓗ**
Cool	Men	Want	Up
Pool	Red	Saw	Sun
Too	Bed	Law	Cup
ⓞⓦ	**ⓞⓨ**	**ⓘ**	**ⓐ**
Cow	Toy	Win	Cat
Now	Boy	Sit	Sad
How	Joy	Kiss	Hat

Portuguese has many nasalized sounds. Whenever you see a tilde (˜) over a vowel, think "nasal". Also, vowels before M and N are usually nasalized. In this book we simply add (ñg) to remind you.

Ⓞñg   ⓞⓦñg   ⓐⓗñg   ⓄⓄñg

The g is not actually pronounced but try to mentally get as close as possible to the nasalized sounds by listening to native speakers.

EPLS CONSONANTS

Consonants are letters like **T**, **B**, and **K**. They are easy to recognize and their pronunciation seldom changes. The following pronunciation guide letters represent some unique Portuguese consonant sounds.

ñg   These **EPLS** letters provide a visual prompt that nasalization is part of the correct pronunciation of the vowel. The g is shown in a lighter tint because although it is part of the nasalization it is **not** actually spoken.

Ɓ   Represents a rolled **r** sound.

R   Pronounced like **r** in **r**ide.

H   Pronounce this letter like the **h** in **h**orse

J   Pronounce this letter like the **j** in **j**eep.

GW   Pronounce these **EPLS** letters like **gu** in La**Gu**ardia Airport or the **gu** in i**gu**ana.

KW   Pronounce these **EPLS** letters like **qu** in **qu**ick and **qu**est.

CH   Pronounce these **EPLS** letters like **ch** in **ch**eap or **ch**eck.

SH   Pronounce these **EPLS** letters like **s** in **sh**ow.

ZH   Pronounce these **EPLS** letters like **s** in mea**s**ure.

PRONUNCIATION TIPS

- Each pronunciation guide word is broken into syllables. Read each word slowly, one syllable at a time, increasing speed as you become more familiar with the system.

- In Portuguese it is important to emphasize certain syllables. This mark (´) over the syllable reminds you to stress that syllable.

- The pronunciation and word choices in this book were chosen for their simplicity and effectiveness.

- In Portuguese there are many nasalized vowel sounds for which there is no equivalent in the English language. EPLS uses the following consonant enhancement to signal you that the vowel is nasalized; (ñg).

- To perfect your Portuguese accent you must listen closely to native speakers and adjust your speech accordingly.

- The Portuguese language has different sounds for the same letter based on the placement of the letter in the word. Variances also occur according to the beginning sound of the word that follows.

- The good news! EPLS has done the work for you and transliterated the correct sound, so all you have to do is start speaking the language. Don't forget the nasalizations!

ICONS USED IN THIS BOOK

KEY WORDS

You will find this icon at the beginning of chapters indicating key words relating to chapter content. These are important words to become familiar with.

PHRASEMAKER

The Phrasemaker icon provides the traveler with a choice of phrases that allows the user to make his or her own sentences.

Say It Right in

BRAZILIAN PORTUGUESE

ESSENTIAL WORDS AND PHRASES

Here are some basic words and phrases that will help you express your needs and feelings in **Portuguese**.

Hello

Oi / Olá

Ō′-EE / Ō-L-ah′

How are you? (polite)

Como vai você?

KŌ′-Moo VĪ VO-Sā′

Very well, thanks.

Muito bem, obrigado. (m)   Muito bem, obrigada. (f)

MWEEng-Too BAng Ō-BREE-Gah-Doo (ah)

Ok / So so

Bem / Mais ou menos

BAng / MĪS o Mē-NOS

Tudo bem?   Tudo bom.

Too-Doo BAng   Too-Doo BOng

You will hear these two phrases used interchangeably in Brazil. They literally mean "Everything well?" and "Everything is good." If a Native Brazilian says one of these phrases to you, then you may respond with the other phrase and vice versa. The phrases above for "How are you?" and "Very well, thanks." are more polite.

Good morning
Bom dia

BOñg JEE-ah

Good afternoon
Boa tarde

BO'ah TahR-JEE

Good evening
Boa noite

BO'ah Noy-CHEE

Good night
Boa noite

BO'ah Noy-CHEE

Good-bye (See you later.)
Até logo

ah-TE' Lah'-Goo

Good-bye
Tchau

CHow

Mr.
Senhor.

SEñg-YOR

Mrs.
Senhora.

SEñg-YO-Rah

Miss.
Senhorita.

SEñg-YO-REE-Tah

Yes

Sim

SEEñg

No	**OK**
Não	Certo
NOWñg	SÊR-Too

Please

Por favor

POR Fah-VOR

Thank you

Obrigado (m)	Obrigada (f)
O-BREE-Gah-Doo	O-BREE-Gah-Dah

You're welcome.

De nada.

JEE Nah-Dah

Excuse me.

Desculpe.

JÊS-KooL-PEE

I'm sorry

Sinto muito

SEEñg-Too MWEEñg-Too

I'm a tourist.

Eu sou turista.

ẽ⃝⓪ SO T⓪-RẼ'S-Tah

I don't speak Portuguese.

Eu não falo Português.

ẽ⃝⓪ Nⓞⓦñg Fah'-L⓪
POR-T⓪-Gẽ'S

Do you speak English?

Você fala inglês?

VO-SA' Fah'L EEñg-GLẽ'S

I don't understand!

Eu não entendo!

ẽ⃝⓪ Nⓞⓦñg EEN-Tẽñg-D⓪

Please repeat.

Repita, por favor.

Hẽ-PEE'-Tah POR Fah-VO'R

More slowly, please.

Por favor, fale mais devagar.

POR Fah-VO'R,
Fah'-LEE MⒾS Jẽ-Vah-Gah'R

FEELINGS

I would like...

Eu gostaria...

ĕ︠oo︡ GO-STah-REE-ah...

I want...

Eu quero...

ĕ︠oo︡ Kĕ-Roo...

I have...

Eu tenho...

ĕ︠oo︡ Tĕñg-Yoo...

I know.   **I don't know.**

Eu sei.   Eu não sei.

ĕ︠oo︡ SA   ĕ︠oo︡ Nowñg SA

I like it.

Eu gosto.

ĕ︠oo︡ GahS-Too

I don't like it.

Eu não gosto.

ĕ︠oo︡ Nowñg GahS-Too

I'm lost.

Estou perdido. (m)   Estou perdida. (f)

ⓔS-TⓄ́ PⓔR-JⓔⒺ́-DⓄⓄ (ⓐⓗ)

We are lost.

Nós estamos perdidos. (m)   perdidas. (f)

NⓐⓗS ⓔS-Tⓐⓗ́-MⓄS PⓔR-JⓔⒺ́-DⓄⓄS
NⓐⓗS ⓔS-Tⓐⓗ́-MⓄS PⓔR-JⓔⒺ́-DⓐⓗS

I'm tired.

Estou cansado. (m)   Estou cansada. (f)

ⓔS-TⓄ́ Kⓐⓗñg-Sⓐⓗ́-DⓄⓄ (ⓐⓗ)

I'm ill.

Estou doente.

ⓔS-TⓄ́ DⓄ-ⓔ́ñg-CHⓔⒺ

I'm hungry.

Tenho fome.

Tⓔñg-YⓄⓄ Fⓐⓗ́-MⓔⒺ

I'm thirsty.

Tenho sede.

Tⓔñg-YⓄⓄ Sⓔ́-JⓔⒺ

I'm happy.

Estou feliz.

ⓔS-TⓄ́ Fⓔ́-LⓔⒺ́S

INTRODUCTIONS

My name is...

Meu nome é...

MⒺⓄ Nⓐ-MⒺ Ⓔ...

Where are you from?

De onde você é?

JⒺ Ⓞñg-JⒺ VⓄ-SⒶ Ⓔ

Do you live here?

Você mora aqui?

VⓄ-SⒶ MⓄ-Rⓐ ⓐ-KⒺ

I just arrived.

Acabo de chegar.

ⓐ-Kⓐ-Bⓞⓞ JⒺ CHⒺ-Gⓐʀ

What hotel are you staying at?

Em que hotel você está?

Ⓔñg KⒺ Ⓞ-TⒺL VⓄ-SⒶ
ⒺS-Tⓐ

I'm at the...hotel.

Estou no hotel...

ⓔS-Tⓞ́ Nⓞⓞ...ⓞTⓔ́L

It was nice to meet you.

Foi um prazer conhecê-lo. (m)

Fⓞⓨ ⓞⓞñg PRⓐⓗ-Zⓔ́R Kⓞ-Nⓔ́-Sⓔ́-Lⓞⓞ

It was nice to meet you.

Foi um prazer conhecê-la. (f)

Fⓞⓨ ⓞⓞñg PRⓐⓗ-Zⓔ́R Kⓞ-Nⓔ́-Sⓔ́-Lⓐⓗ

See you later.

Até mais tarde.

ⓐⓗ-Tⓔ́ MⓐⓗS TⓐⓗR-JⒺⒺ

See you next time.

Até a próxima vez.

ⓐⓗ-Tⓔ́ ⓐⓗ PRⓐⓗ-SⒺⒺ-Mⓐⓗ Vⓔ́S

Good luck!

Boa sorte!

Bⓞ́ⓐⓗ Sⓞ́R-CHⒺⒺ

THE BIG QUESTIONS

Who?

Quem?

K**A**ñg

Who is it?

Quem é?

K**A**ñg Y**ê**

What?

O que?

O K**ê**

What is this?

O que é isto?

O K**ê** **EE**'S-T**oo**

When?

Quando?

KW**ah**ñg-D**oo**

Where?

Onde?

Oñg-J**EE**

Where is...?

Onde é...?

Oñg-JEE ĕ...

Which?

Qual?

KWahL

Why?

Por quê?

POB Kĕ

How?

Como?

KO'-Moo

How much?

Quanto?

KWahñg-Too

How long?

Quanto tempo?

KWahñg-Too TĕM-Poo

ASKING FOR THINGS

The following phrases are valuable for directions, food, help, etc.

I would like...

Eu queria...

ⓔⓞⓞ Kⓔ-Rⓔⓔ-ⓐⓗ...

I need...	**Can you...**
Eu preciso...	Você pode...
ⓔⓞⓞ PRⓔ-Sⓔⓔ-Zⓞⓞ...	Vⓞ-Sⓐ Pⓐⓗ-Jⓔⓔ...

When asking a question it is polite to say "May I ask" and "Thank you."

May I ask?

Posso perguntar?

PⓞS-Sⓞⓞ PⓔR-GⓞⓞN-TⓐⓗR

Thank you.

Obrigado. (m)   Obrigada. (f)

ⓞ-BRⓔⓔ-Gⓐⓗ-Dⓞⓞ (ⓐⓗ)

PHRASEMAKER

I would like...

Quería...

KḖ-RĒE-ah...

▶ **coffee**

café

Kah-Fḗ

▶ **some water**

água

ah-GWah

▶ **ice water**

água gelada

ah-GWah   ZHḖ-Lah-Dah

▶ **the menu**

o cardápio

oo   KahR-Dah-PEEoo

PHRASEMAKER

Here are a few sentences
you can use when you feel
the urge to say **I need**... or **can you**...?

I need...

Eu preciso...

ⓔ⑩ PRⓔ-Sⓔⓔ-Z⑩...

▸ **your help**

da sua ajuda

Dⓐⓗ S⑩ⓐⓗ ⓐⓗ-ZH⑩-Dⓐⓗ

▸ **more money**

de mais dinheiro

Jⓔⓔ MⓘS Dⓔⓔ-Nⓐ-R⑩

▸ **change**

de troco

Jⓔⓔ TRⓞ-K⑩

▸ **a doctor**

de um médico

Jⓔⓔ ⑩ñg Mⓔ-Jⓔⓔ-K⑩

▸ **a lawyer**

de um advogado

Jⓔⓔ ⑩ñg ⓐⓗD-V⑩-Gⓐⓗ-D⑩

PHRASEMAKER

Can you...

Você pode...

VO-SA PaH-JEE...

▸ **help me?**

me ajudar?

MEE aH-ZHoo-DaHR

▸ **give me?**

me dar?

MEE DaHR

▸ **tell me...?**

me dizer...?

MEE JEE-ZeR...

▸ **take me to...?**

me levar a...?

MEE LeH-VaHR aH...

ASKING THE WAY

No matter how independent you are, sooner or later you'll probably have to ask for directions.

Where is...?

Onde é...?

Oñg-JEE ě...

Is it near?

Fica perto?

FEE-Kah PěR-Too

Is it far?

Fica longe?

FEE-Kah LOñg-ZEE

I'm lost.

Estou perdido. (m)   Estou perdida. (f)

ěS-TO PěR-JEE-Doo (ah)

I'm looking for…

Estou procurando...

ěS-TO PRO-Koo-RahN-Doo...

PHRASEMAKER

Where is...

Onde é...

Ⓞñg-JⒺ ⓔ...

▶ **the restroom?**

o banheiro?

⓪ Bⓐñg-YⒶ-Rⓞ

▶ **the telephone?**

o telefone?

⓪ TⓔⓁ-ⓔ-Fⓞ-NⒺ

▶ **the beach?**

a praia?

ⓐ PRⒾ-ⓐ...

▶ **the hotel?**

o hotel?

⓪ Ⓞ-TⓔⓁ...

▶ **the train for...**

o trem para...

⓪ TRⒶñg Pⓐ-Rⓐ...

TIME

What time is it?

Que horas são?

K@ @'-B@S S@ñg

Morning

Manhã

M@ñg-Y@ñg

Noon

Tarde

T@'B-J@

Night

Noite

N@'-CH@

Today

Hoje

@'-ZH@

Tomorrow

Amanhã

@-M@ñg-Y@ñg

This week

Esta semana

ĕS-Tah   Sĕ-Mah-Nah

This month

Este mês

ĕS-CHEE   MĕS

This year

Este ano

ĕS-CHEE   ah-Noo

Now

Agora

ah-GŌ-Rah

Soon

Logo

Lah-Goo

Later

Depois

Dĕ-PoÿS

Never

Nunca

Nooñg-Kah

WHO IS IT?

I

Eu

You

Você

V⊚-S⒜́

You (plural)

Vocês

V⊚-S⒜́S

He / she

Ele / Ela

⒠́-L㊾ / ⒠́-L⒜

We

Nós

N⒜S

They

Eles (m) / Elas (f)

⒠́-L㊾S / ⒠́-L⒜S

WHO IS IT?

In Portuguese all things are masculine or feminine. It is strange to think of a car, chair or piano as masculine or feminine; however, EPLS makes it easy by demonstrating this in a simple way as shown below. The **(m)** following the word **perdido** signals masculine and the **(f)** following **perdida** signals feminine. You will notice that most masculine words will end in **(o)** and feminine words will end in **(a)**. Where there is room the entire phrase will be written in the EPLS transliteration, but in most cases you will see the word written in masculine pronunciation followed with the feminine sound in parenthesis as shown below.

Example:

I'm lost.

Estou perdido. (m)   Estou perdida. (f)

ⓔS-TⓄ PⓔR-JⒺⒺ-DⓄⓄ (ⓐⓗ)

If a word is singular or plural it will be indicated by an (s) for singular and (pl) for plural; e.g., masculine singular (m,s) masculine plural (m,pl) feminine singular (f,s) and feminine plural (f,pl) respectively.

(m) Masculine   (m,s) Masculine singular

                    (m,pl) Masculine plural

(f) Feminine   (f,s) Feminine singular

                    (f,pl) Feminine plural

THIS, THAT AND THESE

The equivalents of **this, that,** and **these** are as follows.

This	**This**	**This** (thing)
Este (m)	Esta (f)	Isto (n)
ⓔS-CHⒺⒺ	ⓔS-Tⓐⓗ	ⒺⒺS-Tⓞⓞ

This is mine.

Este é meu. (m,s)

ⓔS-CHⒺⒺ ⓔ Mⓔⓞⓞ

This is mine.

Esta é minha. (f,s)

ⓔS-Tⓐⓗ ⓔ MⒺⒺñg-Yⓐⓗ

That	**That**	**That** (thing)
Aquele (m)	Aquela (f)	Aquilo (n)
ⓐⓗ-Kⓔ-LⒺⒺ	ⓐⓗ-Kⓔ-Lⓐⓗ	ⓐⓗ-KⒺⒺ-Lⓞⓞ

That is mine.

Aquilo é meu. (m,s)

ⓐⓗ-KⒺⒺ-Lⓞⓞ ⓔ Mⓔⓞⓞ

That is mine.

Aquila é minhas. (f,s)

ⓐⓗ-Kⓔ-Lⓐⓗ ⓔ MⒺⒺñg-Yⓐⓗ

THIS, THAT AND THESE

In Brazilian Portuguese there is no equivalent for "it" used in the English language.

These

Estes (m) / Estas (f)

ⓔS-CHⒺS / ⓔS-TⓐS

These are mine.

Estes são meus. (m,pl)

ⓔS-CHⒺS Sⓞⓦñg MⓔⓄⓄS

These are mine.

Estas são minhas. (f,pl)

ⓔS-TⓐS Sⓞⓦñg MⒺñg-YⓐS

USEFUL OPPOSITES

Near	**Far**
Perto	Longe
PĔR-Too	LOñg-ZHEE
Here	**There**
Aqui	Lá
ah-KEE	Lah
Left	**Right**
Esquerda	Direita
ĕS-KĔR-Dah	JEE-RA-Tah
A little	**A lot**
Um pouco	Muito
ooñg PO-Koo	MWEEñg-Too
More	**Less**
Mais	Menos
MIS	MĔ-NOS
Big	**Small**
Grande	Pequeno (m)
GRahñg-JEE	Pequena (f)
	PEE-KĔN-oo
	PEE-KĔN-ah

Open	**Closed**
Aberto (m) Aberta (f)	Fechado (m) Fechada (f)
ah-BĚR-Too (ah)	FĚ-SHah-Doo (ah)

Cheap	**Expensive**
Barato (m) Barata (f)	Caro (m) Cara (f)
Bah-Rah-Too (ah)	Kah-Roo (ah)

Clean	**Dirty**
Limpo (m) Limpa (f)	Sujo (m) Suja (f)
LĚM-Poo (ah)	Soo-ZHoo (ah)

Good	**Bad**
Bom (m) Boa (f)	Mau (m) Má (f)
BOñg BO'ah	Mow Mah

Vacant	**Occupied**
Vazio (m) Vazia (f)	Ocupado (m) Ocupada (f)
Vah-ZEE-oo (ah)	O-Koo-Pah-Doo (ah)

Right	**Wrong**
Certo (m) Certa (f)	Errado (m) Errada (f)
SĚR-Too (ah)	Ě-Hah-Doo (ah)

WORDS OF ENDEARMENT

I like you.

Eu gosto de você.

ⓔⓞⓞ Gⓐⓗ'S-Tⓞⓞ Jⓔⓔ Vⓞ-Sⓐ'

I love you.

Eu amo você.

ⓔⓞⓞ ⓐⓗ'-Mⓞⓞ Vⓞ-Sⓐ'

I love Brazil.

Eu amo o Brasil.

ⓔⓞⓞ ⓐⓗ'-Mⓞⓞ ⓞⓞ BⓇⓐⓗ-Sⓔⓔ'L

My friend (to a male)

Meu amigo

Mⓔⓞⓞ ⓐⓗ-Mⓔⓔ'-Gⓞⓞ

My friend (to a female)

Minha amiga

Mⓔⓔñg-Yⓐⓗ ⓐⓗ-Mⓔⓔ'-Gⓐⓗ

Kiss me!

Me beije!

Mⓔⓔ Bⓐ'-ZHⓔⓔ

WORDS OF ANGER

What do you want?

O que é que você quer?

Ⓞ Kⓔ̃ KⒺⒺ VⓄ-SⒶ́ Kⓔ̃R

Leave me alone!

Me deixe em paz!

Mⓔ̃ DⒶ́-SHⒺⒺ ⓔ̃M PⓐS

Go away!

Vai embora!

VⒾ ⓔ̃M-BⓄ́-Rⓐ

Stop bothering me!

Não me aborreça!

Nⓞⓦñg MⒺⒺ ⓐ-BⓄ-Hⓔ̃-Sⓐ

Be quiet!

Silencio!

SⒺⒺ-LⒺⒺñg-SⒺⒺⓄ

That's enough!

Chega!

SHⓔ̃-Gⓐ

COMMON EXPRESSIONS

When you are at a loss for words but have the feeling you should say something, try one of these!

No problem.

Não há problema.

N@ñg @ PR@-BL@-M@

Congratulations!

Parabéns!

P@-R@-B@ñgS

Good Luck!

Boa sorte!

B@@ S@R-CH@

Welcome!

Bem vindo! (m) / Bem vinda! (f)

B@ñg V@ñg-D@ / B@ñg V@ñg-D@

Cheers!

Saúde!

S@-@-J@

Wow!

Nossa!

NŌ-S@h

Wonderful!

Ótimo!

@h-CH€€-M@o

Fantastic!

Fantástico!

F@hN-T@hS-CH€€-K@o

My goodness!

Meu Deus!

M@ë@o D@ëŌS

Who knows!

Quem sabe!

K@ñg S@h-B€€

That's too bad. / What a shame.

Que pena.

K€€ P@ë-N@h

Never mind!

Não importa!

N@oñg €€ñg-PŌR-T@h

USEFUL COMMANDS

Stop!

Pare!

P@-R@

Go!

Vá!

V@

Wait!

Espere!

@S-P@-R@

Hurry!

Corra!

K@-H@

Slow down!

Devagar!

J@-V@-G@R

Come here!

Venha cá!

V@ñg-Y@ K@

EMERGENCIES

Fire!

Fogo!

FŌ´-G⓪

Help!

Socorro!

S⓪-KŌ´-H⓪

Emergency!

Emergência!

ⓔ´-Mⓔ̆R-ZHⒶ́ñg-SⒺⒺ-ⓐ

Call the police!

Chame a polícia!

SHⓐ́-MⓔⒺ ⓐ P⓪-LⒺ́Ⓔ-SⒺⒺ-ⓐ

Call a doctor!

Chame um médico!

SHⓐ́-MⓔⒺ ⓪ñg Mⓔ̆´-JⒺⒺ-K⓪

Call an ambulance!

Chame uma ambulância!

SHⓐ́-MⓔⒺ ⓪ñg
ⓐñg-B⓪-Lⓐ́ñg-SⒺⒺ-ⓐ

ARRIVAL

Passing through customs should be easy since there are usually agents available who speak English. You may be asked how long you intend to stay and if you have anything to declare.

- Have your passport ready.

- All travelers must complete and sign an Accompanied Baggage Declaration form.

- Be sure all documents are up-to-date.

- While in a foreign country, it is wise to keep receipts for everything you buy.

- Be aware that many countries will charge a departure tax when you leave. Your travel agent should be able to find out if this affects you.

- If you have connecting flights, be sure to reconfirm them in advance.

- Make sure your luggage is clearly marked inside and out and always keep an eye on it when in public places.

- Take valuables and medicines in carry-on bags.

KEY WORDS

Baggage

Bagagem

B@-G@-ZH@ñg

Customs

Alfândega

@L-F@ñg-J€-G@

Documents

Documentos

D@-K∞-M€ñg-T∞S

Passport

Passaporte

P@S-S@-P⊙B-CH€

Porter

Carregador

K@-H€-G@-D⊙B

Taxi

Táxi

T@K-S€

USEFUL PHRASES

Here is my passport.

Aqui está meu passaporte.

ah-KEE eS-Tah Me-oo
PahS-Sah-POR-CHEE

I have nothing to declare.

Não tenho nada a declarar.

Nowñg Teñ-Yoo Nah-Dah
ah De-KLah-RahR

I'm here on business.

Eu estou aqui a negócios.

e-oo eS-TO ah-KEE ah
Ne-GO-SEE-ooS

I'm here on vacation.

Eu estou aqui de férias.

e-oo eS-TO ah-KEE JEE Fe-REE-ahS

Is there a problem?

Tem algum problema?

Teñ ahL-Gooñg PRO-BLe-Mah

PHRASEMAKER

I'll be staying...

Vou ficar...

VŌ FEE-KahR...

▶ **one night**

uma noite

OO-Mah NOY-CHEE

▶ **two nights**

duas noites

DOO-ahS NOY-CHEES

▶ **one week**

uma semana

OO-Mah Sĕ-Mah-Nah

▶ **two weeks**

duas semanas

DOO-ahS
Sĕ-Mah-NahS

USEFUL PHRASES

Where is baggage claim?

Onde posso pegar as minhas malas?.

Oñg-JEE PO'S-Soo PĒ-GahR ahS
MEEN-YahS Mah-LahS

I need a porter.

Eu preciso de um carregador.

Ēoo PRĒ-SEE-Zoo JEE ooñg
Kah-HĒ-Gah-DO'R

These are my bags.

Estas são as minhas malas.

ĒS-TahS Sowñg ahS
MEEN-YahS Mah-LahS

I'm missing a bag.

Está faltando uma mala.

ĒS-Tah FahL-Tahñg-Doo
oo-Mah Mah-Lah

Thank you. This is for you.

Obrigado. (m) Obrigada. (f) Isto é para você.

O-BREE-Gah-Doo (ah)
EE'S-Too Ē Pah-Rah VO-Sa

PHRASEMAKER

Where is...

Onde é...

Ⓞ́ñg-JⒺ Ⓔ̌...

▸ **customs?**

a alfândega?

ⓐ ⓐL-Fⓐñg-JⒺ-Gⓐ

▸ **the restroom?**

o banheiro?

⓪ Bⓐñg-YⒶ́-RⓄ

▸ **the money exchange?**

a casa de câmbio?

ⓐ Kⓐ́-Zⓐ JⒺ Kⓐ́M-BⒺ-⓪

▸ **the taxi stand?**

o ponto de táxi?

⓪ PⓄ́ñg-T⓪ JⒺ Tⓐ́K-SⒺ

▸ **the bus stop?**

o ponto de ônibus?

⓪ PⓄ́ñg-T⓪ JⒺ Ⓞ́-NⒺ-B⓪S

Note: At the end of the sentence, raise the tone of your voice slightly indicating a question.

HOTEL
SURVIVAL

A wide selection of
accommodations
is available in Brazil.
They range from elite
modern hotels to smaller
hotels, quest houses (family
owned and usually include breakfast), to
rental holiday homes in the country.

- Make reservations well in advance and request the address of the hotel to be written in Portuguese as most taxi drivers do not speak English.

- Accommodations are rated according to amenities offered.

- Do not leave valuables or cash in your room when you are not there!

- Electrical items like blow-dryers may need an adapter and/or connector. Your hotel may be able to provide one, but to be safe, take one with you.

- It is a good idea to make sure you give your room number to persons you expect to call you. This can avoid confusion with western names.

KEY WORDS

Hotel

Hotel

Ⓞ-Tⓔ́L

Bellman

Carregador

Kⓐⓗ-Hⓔ́-Gⓐⓗ-DⓄ́R

Maid

Arrumadeira

ⓐⓗ-HⓄ-Mⓐⓗ-Dⓐ́-Rⓐⓗ

Message

Recado / mensagem

Hⓔ́-Kⓐⓗ-Dⓞⓞ / MⒶñg-Sⓐⓗ́-ZHⓔ́ñg

Reservation

Reserva

Hⓔ́-Zⓔ́R-Vⓐⓗ

Room service

Serviço de quarto

Sⓔ́R-VⒺⒺ́-Sⓞⓞ JⒺⒺ KWⓐⓗ́R-Tⓞⓞ

CHECKING IN

My name is...

Meu nome é...

Mᴇ̃ᴏᴏ Nᴀ̃ʜ-Mᴇᴇ ᴇ̃...

I have a reservation.

Tenho reserva.

Tᴀ̃ñg-Yᴏᴏ Hᴇ̃-Sᴇ̃ʀ-Vᴀʜ

Have you any vacancies?

Tem vaga?

Tᴀ̃ñg Vᴀʜ-Gᴀʜ

What is the charge per night?

Quanto é a diária?

KWᴀʜñg-Tᴏᴏ ᴇ̃ ᴀʜ Jᴇᴇ-ᴀʜ-Rᴇᴇ-ᴀʜ

Is there room service?

Tem serviço de quarto?

Tᴀ̃ñg Sᴇ̃ʀ-Vᴇᴇ-Sᴏᴏ Jᴇᴇ KWᴀʜʀ-Tᴏᴏ

My room key, please.

Minha chave, por favor.

Mᴇᴇñg-Yᴀʜ SHᴀʜ-Vᴇᴇ Pᴏʀ Fᴀʜ-Vᴏʀ

PHRASEMAKER

I would like a room...

Eu quero um quarto...

ⓔⓞⓞ KⒶ'-Rⓞⓞ ⓞⓞñg KWⓐ'R-Tⓞⓞ...

▶ **with a bath**

com banheiro

KⓄñg Bⓐñg-YⒶ'-Rⓞⓞ

▶ **with one bed**

com uma cama

KⓄñg ⓞⓞ'-Mⓐ Kⓐ'-Mⓐ

▶ **with two beds**

com duas camas

KⓄñg Dⓞⓞ'-ⓐS Kⓐ'-MⓐS

▶ **with a shower**

com chuveiro

KⓄñg SHⓞⓞ-VⒶ'-Rⓞⓞ

▶ **with a view**

com vista

KⓄñg VⒺⒺ'-STⓤ

USEFUL PHRASES

My room key, please.

Minha chave por favor.

MⒺ́ñg-Y⒜h SH⒜h́-VⒺ PⓄB F⒜h-VⓄ́B

Are there any messages for me?

Tem algum recado para mim?

T⒜ñg ⒜hL-Gⓞⓞñg HⒺ̃-K⒜h́-Dⓞⓞ
P⒜h́-B⒜h MⒺ́ñg

Where is the dining room?

Onde é o restaurante?

Ⓞ́ñg-JⒺⒺ Ⓔ̃ ⓞⓞ HⒺ̃-STⓞⱳ-B⒜hñg-CHⒺⒺ

Are meals included?

As refeições estão incluídas?

⒜hS HⒺ̃-FⒶ-SⓞⱴñgS Ⓔ̃S-Tⓞⱳñg
ⒺⒺN-KLⓞⓞ-ⒺⒺ́-D⒜hS

What time is breakfast?

A que hora é o cafe da manhã?

⒜h KⒶ Ⓞ́-B⒜h Ⓔ̃ ⓞⓞ
K⒜h-FⒺ̃́ D⒜h M⒜hñg-Y⒜h́

What time is dinner?

A que hora é o jantar?

⒜h KⒶ Ⓞ́-B⒜h Ⓔ̃ ⓞⓞ ZH⒜hN-T⒜h́B

PHRASEMAKER
(WAKE UP CALL)

Please wake me at...

Por favor, me acorde às...

P⊚R F⟨ah⟩-V⊙R M⟨ee⟩ ⟨ah⟩-K⊙R-D⟨ee⟩ ⟨ah⟩S...

▸ **6:00 a.m.**
seis da manhã
S⟨a⟩S D⟨ah⟩ M⟨ah⟩ñg-Y⟨ah⟩

▸ **6:30 a.m.**
seis e meia
S⟨a⟩S ⟨ee⟩ M⟨a⟩⟨ah⟩

▸ **7:00 a.m.**
sete horas
S⟨ě⟩-CH⟨ee⟩ ⊙-R⟨ah⟩S

▸ **7:30 a.m.**
sete e meia
S⟨ě⟩-CH⟨ee⟩ M⟨a⟩-⟨ah⟩

▸ **8:00 a.m.**
oito horas
⟨oy⟩-T⟨oo⟩ ⊙-R⟨ah⟩S

▸ **9:00 a.m.**
nove horas
N⊙-V⟨ee⟩ ⊙-R⟨ah⟩S

PHRASEMAKER

I need...

Eu preciso...

ⓔⓞ PRⓔ-Sⓔ́-Zⓞ...

▸ **a babysitter**

de uma babá

Jⓔ ⓞ́-Mⓐ Bⓐ-Bⓐ́

▸ **a bellman**

de um carregador

Jⓔ ⓞñg Kⓐ-Hⓔ-Gⓐ-DⓄ́R

▸ **more blankets**

de mais cobertores

Jⓔ Mⓞ́S KⓄ-Bⓔ́R-TⓄ́-Rⓔ́S

▸ **a hotel safe**

de um cofre

Jⓔ ⓞñg KⓄ́-FRⓔ

▸ **ice cubes**

de cubos de gelo

Jⓔ KⓄ́-Bⓞ́S Dⓔ ZHⓔ́-Lⓞ

▸ **an extra key**

de outra chave

JEE O'-TRah SHah'-VEE

▸ **a maid**

de uma arrumadeira

JEE oo'-Mah ah-Hoo-Mah-DA'-Rah

▸ **the manager**

do gerente do hotel

DO ZHĕ-Rĕñg-CHEE Doo O-TĕL

▸ **clean sheets**

de lençóis limpos

JEE LĕN-Soy'S LEEñg-PooS

▸ **soap**

de sabonete

JEE Sah-BO-Nĕ'-CHEE

▸ **toilet paper**

de papel higiênico

JEE Pah-PĕL EE-ZHEE-ĕ'-NEE-Koo

▸ **more towels**

de mais toalhas

JEE MOS TOah'L-YahS

PHRASEMAKER

(PROBLEMS)

There is no...

Não tem...

N⬤ñg T⬤ñg...

▶ **electricity**

eletricidade

⬤-L⬤K-TR⬤-S⬤-D⬤-J⬤

▶ **heat**

aquecimento

⬤-K⬤-S⬤-M⬤N-T⬤

▶ **hot water**

água quente

⬤-GW⬤ K⬤N-CH⬤

▶ **light**

luz

L⬤S

▶ **toilet paper**

papel higiênico

P⬤-P⬤L ⬤-ZH⬤-⬤-N⬤-K⬤

PHRASEMAKER

(SPECIAL NEEDS)

Is there...

Tem...

T⒜ñg...

▶ **an elevator?**

elevador?

ⓔ-Lⓔ-V⒜-DⓄ'B

▶ **a ramp?**

rampa?

H⒜ñg-P⒜

▶ **a wheel chair?**

cadeira de rodas?

K⒜-D⒜'-B⒜ JⒺ HⓄ'-D⒜S

▶ **facilities for the disabled?**

facilidades para incapacitados?

F⒜-SⒺ-LⒺ-D⒜'-JⒺS P⒜'-B⒜
Ⓔñg-K⒜-P⒜-SⒺ-T⒜'-DⓄⓄS

CHECKING OUT

The bill, please.

A conta por favor.

ⓐ KⓄñg-Tⓐ PⓄB Fⓐ-VⓄB

Is this bill correct?

Esta conta está certa?

ⓔS-Tⓐ KⓄN-Tⓐ ⓔS-Tⓐ SⓔB-Tⓐ

Do you accept credit cards?

Aceita cartão de crédito?

ⓐ-SⒶ-Tⓐ KⓐB-Tⓞⓦñg JⒺ
KBⓔ-JⒺ-Tⓞⓞ

Could you have my luggage brought down?

Pode mandar trazer a minha bagagem
para baixo?

PⓄ-JⒺ Mⓐñg-DⓐB
TBⓐ-ZⓔB ⓐ MⒺñg-Yⓐ
Bⓐ-Gⓐ-ZHⒶñg Pⓐ-Bⓐ BⒾ-SHⓞⓞ

Please call a taxi.

Por favor, chame um táxi.

POR Fah-VOR SHah-MEE
oong Tah'K-SEE

I had a very good time!

Me diverti muito!

MEE JEE-VER-CHEE MooYng-Too

Thanks for everything.

Obrigado por tudo. (m)   Obrigada por tudo. (f)

O-BREE-Gah'-Doo POR Too-Doo
O-BREE-Gah'-Dah POR Too-Doo

See you next time.

Até a próxima vez.

ah-TE' ah PRah'S-SEE-Mah VeS

Good-bye

Até logo.

ah-TE' LO'-Goo

RESTAURANT SURVIVAL

As a cosmopolitan country, the majority of Brazil's main cities offer tourists a variety of Brazilian dishes. Churrasco (barbecue) restaurants are wonderful to try. Rodízio restaurants serve a variety of meats continuously. The most common dishes in Brazil include meats, rice and black beans (Feijão).

- Although Brazil is famous for being the largest coffee producer in the world, the national drink is Cachaça, a sugar cane rum.

- Lunch and dinner times vary; however, dinner is served much later in Brazil than in the US. Also, Brazilian etiquette requires that you complete your meal or drink at the restaurant or snack bar (not on the run).

- Tipping is usually a standard 10% which in most restaurants is included in the bill. If you see "Serviço não incluído" then the service charge has not been added.

KEY WORDS

Breakfast

Café da manhã

K@b-F@-D@b M@bñg-Y@b

Lunch

Almoço

@bL-M@-S@

Dinner

Jantar

ZH@bñg-T@bR

Waiter

Garçom

G@bR-S@ñg

Waitress

Garçonete

G@bR-S@-N@-CH@

Restaurant

Restaurante

H@-ST@-R@bñg-CH@

USEFUL PHRASES

A table for...

Uma mesa para...

oo-Mah Mē-Zah Pah-Rah...

2	4	6
dois	quatro	seis
Doys	QWah-TRoo	SAS

The menu, please.

O cardápio, por favor.

oo KahR-Dah-PEEoo POR Fah-VOR

Separate checks, please.

Contas separadas, por favor.

KOñg-TahS Sē-Pah-Rah-DahS
POR Fah-VOR

We are in a hurry.

Nós estamos com pressa.

NahS ēS-Tah-MooS KOñg PRēS-Sah

What do you recommend?

O que você recomenda?

oo KEE VO-SA
Rē-KO-Mēñg-Dah

Please bring me...

Por favor, traga...

POR Fah-VOR TRah-Gah...

Please bring us...

Por favor, traga...

POR Fah-VOR TRah-Gah...

I'm hungry.

Estou com fome.

EES-TO KOñg FO-MEE

I'm thirsty.

Estou com sede.

EES-TO KOñg SE-JEE

Is service included? (tip)

A gorjeta está incluído?

ah GOR-ZHE-Tah eS-Tah
EEñg-KLoo-EE-Doo

The bill, please.

A conta por favor.

ah KOñg-Tah POR Fah-VOR

PHRASEMAKER

Ordering beverages is easy and a great way to practice your Portuguese! In many foreign countries you will have to request ice with your drinks.

Please bring me...

Por favor, traga...

POB F@-V©B TB@-G@...

▸ **Coffee**

Café

K@-F©

▸ **Tea**

Chá

SH@

▸ **with cream**

com creme

K©ñg KB©-M©©

▸ **with sugar**

com açúcar

K©ñg @-S©-K@

▸ **with ice**

com gelo

K©ñg ZH©-L©

▸ **with lemon**

com limão

K©ñg L©-M©ñg

Soft drinks

Refrigerantes

HÊ-FRĬ-GÊ-RahN-CHEES

Milk

Leite

LÂ-CHEE

Hot chocolate

Chocolate quente

SHŎ-KŎ-Lah-CHEE   KÊN-CHEE

Juice

Suco

SOO-KOO

Orange juice

Suco de laranja

SOO-KOO JEE Lah-RahÑg-ZHah

Ice water

Água gelada

ah-GWah ZHÊ-Lah-Dah

Mineral water

Água mineral

ah-GWah MEE-NÊ-ROW

AT THE BAR

Bartender

Garçom

G@B-S©ñg

The wine list, please.

Por favor, a carta de vinhos.

P©B F@-V©B @h K@R-T@h
J©© V©ñg-Y©S

Cocktail

coquetel

K©-K©©-T@L

With ice

com gelo

K©ñg ZH©-L©©

Straight

Puro (m)   Pura (f)

P©©-B©©   P©©-B@h

With lemon

Com limão

K©ñg L©©-M©©ñg

PHRASEMAKER

I would like a glass of...

Eu quero um copo de...

(ⓔ)ⓞⓞ KⒶ´-Ⓡⓞⓞ ⓞⓞñg KⓄ´-Pⓞⓞ Jⓔⓔ...

▸ **champagne**

champanhe

SHⒶⓜM-PⒶⓐñg-Yⓔ

▸ **beer**

cerveja

Sⓔ-Ⓡ-Vⓔ´-ZHⒶⓐ

▸ **wine**

vinho

Vⓔⓔ´ñg-Yⓞⓞ

▸ **red wine**

vinho tinto

Vⓔⓔ´ñg-Yⓞⓞ Tⓔⓔ´ñg-Tⓞⓞ

▸ **white wine**

vinho branco

Vⓔⓔ´ñg-Yⓞⓞ BⓇⒶⓐñg-Kⓞⓞ

ORDERING BREAKFAST

In Brazil breakfast is usually simple, consisting of coffee, milk, toast and sometimes meat, cheese and fresh fruit.

Bread	**Toast**
Pão	Torrada
P(ow)ñg	T(o)-H(ah)-D(ah)

with butter

com manteiga

K(o)ñg M(ah)N-T(a)́-G(ah)

with jam

com geléia

K(o)ñg ZH(e)̃-L(a)́-(ah)

Cereal

cereal

S(e)̃-R(ee)-(ow)́L

PHRASEMAKER

I would like...

Eu quero...

EE-O KE-Roo...

▶ **two eggs**

dois ovos

DoyS O-VooS

▶ **scrambled**

ovo mexido

O-Voo ME-SHEE-Doo

▶ **fried**   ▶ **fried**

frito (m) frita (f)   fritos (m,pl) fritas (f,pl)

FREE-Too (ah)   FREE-TooS (ahS)

▶ **with bacon**

com bacon or com toucinho

KOng BA-KOng / KOng TO-SEE-NO

▶ **with ham**

com presunto

KOng PRE-SooN-Too

▶ **with potatoes**

com batatas

KOng Bah-Tah-TahS

LUNCH AND DINNER

On the following pages you will
find lists of foods you are familiar
with, along with other information
such as basic utensils and preparation
instructions.

I would like...

Eu queria...

ⓔⓞⓞ Kⓔ-Rⓔⓔ-ⓐⓗ...

We would like...

Nós queremos...

NⓐⓗS Kⓔ-Rⓔ-MⓞⓞS...

Bring us...please

Traga, por favor...

TRⓐⓗ-Gⓐⓗ...POR Fⓐⓗ-VOR

The lady would like...

A senhora quer...

ⓐⓗ Sⓔñ-YO-Rⓐⓗ KⓔR...

The gentleman would like...

O senhor quer...

ⓞⓞ Sⓔñ-YOR KⓔR...

STARTERS

Appetizers

Aperitivos

@-P@R-@-CH@-V@S

Bread and butter

Pão e manteiga

P@ñg @ M@N-T@-G@

Cheese

Queijo

K@-ZH@

Fruit

Fruta

FR@-T@

Salad

Salada

S@-L@-D@

Soup

Sopa

S@-P@

MEATS

Bacon

Bacon

B@-K◎ñg

Beef

Carne de vaca

K@B-N€€ J€€ V@-K@

Beef steak

Bife

B€€-F€€

Ham

Presunto

PB◉-S◎N-T◎

Lamb

Cordeiro

K◎B-D@-B◎

Pork

Porco

P◎B-K◎

Veal

Vitela

V€€-T◉L-@

POULTRY

Baked chicken

Frango assado

FR@ñg-G⊚ @h-S@h'D-⊚

Broiled chicken

Frango grelhado

FR@ñg-G⊚ GR@L-Y@h'-D⊚

Fried chicken

Frango frito

FR@ñg-G⊚ FR@E'-T⊚

Duck

Pato

P@h'-T⊚

Goose

Ganso

G@h'ñg-S⊚

Turkey

Peru

P@'-R⊚'

SEAFOOD

Fish
Peixe

P@-SH㋵

Lobster
Lagosta

L@-G㋡S-T@

Oysters
Ostras

㋡S-TR@S

Salmon
Salmão

S@L-M㋡ñg

Shrimp
Camarão

K@-M@-R㋡ñg

Trout
Truta

TR㊊-T@

Tuna
Atum

@-T㊊ñg

OTHER ENTREES

Sandwich

Sanduíche

SⓐN-Dⓞⓞ-Wⓔⓔ´-SHⓔ

Hot dog

Cachorro quente

Kⓐ-SHⓄ´-Hⓞⓞ Kⓔ̃ñg-CHⓔ

Hamburger

Hambúrguer

ⓐñg-Bⓞⓞ´-Gⓔ̃R

French fries

Batata frita

Bⓐ-Tⓐ´-Tⓐ FRⓔⓔ´-Tⓐ

Pasta

Macarrão

Mⓐ-Kⓐ-Hⓞⓦ´ñg

Pizza

Pizza

Pⓔⓔ´T-Sⓐ

VEGETABLES

Carrots

Cenouras

S℮-NO-Rahs

Corn

Milho

MEEL-Yoo

Mushrooms

Cogumelos

KO-Goo-ME-Loos

Onions

Cebolas

S℮-BO-Lahs

Potato

Batata

Bah-Tah-Tah

Rice

Arroz

ah-HOS

Tomato

Tomate

TO-Mah-CHEE

FRUITS

Apple

Maçã

Mah-Sahñg

Banana

Banana

Bah-Nah-Nah

Grapes

Uvas

oo-Vahs

Lemon

Limão

LEE-Mowñg

Orange

Laranja

Lah-Rahñg-ZHah

Strawberry

Morango

MO-Rahñg-Goo

Watermelon

Melancia

Mё-Lahñg-SEE-ah

DESSERT

Dessert

Sobremesa

SO-BREE-ME-Zah

Apple pie

Torta de maçã

TOR-Tah JEE Mah-Sahñg

Cherry pie

Torta de cereja

TOR-Tah JEE Se-Re-ZHah

Pastries

Doces

DO-SEES

Pastries

Massa folhada

MahS-Sah FOL-Yah-Dah

Candy

Balas

Bah-LahS

Ice cream

Sorvete

SOB-Vě-CHEE

Ice cream cone

Sorvete de casquinha

SOB-Vě-CHEE JEE KahS-KEEñg-Yah

Chocolate

Chocolate

SHO-KO-Lah-CHEE

Strawberry

Morango

MO-Bahñg-Goo

Vanilla

Baunilha

Bow-NEEL-Yah

CONDIMENTS

Butter
Manteiga

MⓐN-TⒶ-Gⓐ

Ketchup
Ketchup / molho de tomate

Kⓔ-CHⓄ-Pⓔ / MⓄ-LYⓄ Jⓔ TⓄ-Mⓐ-CHⓔ

Mayonnaise
Maionese

M①-YⓄ-Nⓔ-Zⓔ

Mustard
Mostarda

MⓄS-TⓐR-Dⓐ

Salt	Pepper
Sal	Pimenta
Sⓞ	Pⓔ-Mⓔñg-Tⓐ

Sugar
Açúcar

ⓐ-SⓄ-KⓐR

Vinegar	Oil
Vinagre	Óleo
Vⓔ-Nⓐ-GRⓔ	ⓐL-YⓄ

SETTINGS

A cup

Uma xícara

oo-Mah SHEE-Keĕ-Bah

A glass

Um copo

ooñg KO-Poo

A spoon

Uma colher

oo-Mah Koo-L-Yeĕ-B

A fork

Um garfo

ooñg Gah-B-Foo

A knife

Uma faca

oo-Mah Fah-Kah

A plate

Um prato

ooñg PBah-Too

A napkin

Um guardanapo

ooñg GWah-B-Dah-Nah-Poo

HOW DO YOU WANT IT COOKED?

Baked
Assado (m) Assada (f)

ⓐhS-Sⓐh-Dⓞⓞ (ⓐh)

Broiled
Grelhado (m) Grelhada (f)

GRⓔL-Yⓐh-Dⓞⓞ (ⓐh)

Steamed
No vapor

Nⓞⓞ Vⓐh-PⓄR

Fried
Frito (m) Frita (f)

FRⒺⒺ-Tⓞⓞ (ⓐh)

Rare
Mal passado (m)   Mal passada (f)

Mⓐh L Pⓐh S-Sⓐh-Dⓞⓞ (ⓐh)

Medium
Médio (m)

Mⓔ-Jⓞⓞ

Média (f)

Mⓔ-Jⓐh

Well done
Bem passado (m)

BⒶñg Pⓐh-Sⓐh-Dⓞⓞ

Bem passada (f)

BⒶñg Pⓐh-Sⓐh-Dⓐh

PROBLEMS

I didn't order this.

Eu não pedi isto.

ẽoo Nowñg Pẽ-JEE EES-Too

Is the bill correct?

A conta está certa?

ah KOñg-Tah ẽS-Tah SẽR-Tah

Please bring me.

Traga, por favor...

TRah-Gah POR Fah-VOR...

PRAISE

Thank you for the delicious meal.

Obrigado (m)   Obrigada (f)
 pela refeição deliciosa.

O-BREE-Gah-Doo / O-BREE-Gah-Dah
Pẽ-Lah Hẽ-FA-Sowñg
Dẽ-LEES-YO-Zah

GETTING AROUND

Getting around in a foreign
country can be an adventure
in itself! Taxi and bus drivers.
do not always speak English, so
it is essential to be able to give
simple directions. The words
and phrases in this chapter will
help you get where you're going.

- Transportation in major cities in Brazil is good and includes intercity buses, local buses, taxis, and subways. However, it should be noted that the subways are not extensive. Local buses connect the city and are economical.

- Taxis can be hailed on the streets; they are yellow taxis with a blue stripe. Radio taxis can be found at airports and hotels and are metered or charge a flat rate (which is a bit more expensive).

- In some cities there is a charge for help with baggage.

- Have a map or the address you want to go to written down in Portuguese.

- Remember to take a business card from your hotel to give to the taxi driver on your return.

KEY WORDS

Airport

Aeroporto

ah-ē-RO-POR-Too

Bus Station

Estação rodoviária

ēS-Tah-Sowñg HO-DO-VEE-ahR-EEah

Bus Stop

Ponto de ônibus

PON-Too JEE O-NEE-BooS

Car Rental Agency

Agência de aluguel de carro

ah-ZHAN-SEEah JEE ahL-oo-GēL
JEE Kah-Hoo

Taxi Stand

Ponto de táxi

PON-Too JEE TahK-SEE

Train Station

Estação ferroviária

ēS-Tah-Sowñg Fē-HO-VEE-ahR-EEah

AIR TRAVEL

Airport

Aeroporto

ah-ē-RO-POR-Too

Departures

Partidas

PahR-CHEE-DahS

Flight number

Número de vôo

Noo-MēR-oo JEE Voo

Airline

Linha aérea

LEEN-Yah ah-ēR-Yah

First class

Primeira classe

PREE-MA-Bah KLah-SEE

Gate

Portão

POR-TOñg

Ticket

Passagem

Pah-Sah-ZHAñg

PHRASEMAKER

I would like a seat...

Eu quero um lugar...

ⓔⓞⓞ KⒶ́-Rⓞⓞ ⓞⓞñg Lⓞⓞ-Gⓐⓗ́R...

▶ **in first class**

na primeira classe

Nⓐⓗ PRⒺⒺ-MⒶ́-Rⓐⓗ KLⓐⓗ́-SⒺⒺ

▶ **next to the window**

perto da janela

PⒺ̈́R-Tⓞⓞ Dⓐⓗ ZHⓐⓗ-NⒺ̈́-Lⓐⓗ

▶ **on the aisle**

no corredor

NⓄ KⓄ-HⒺ̈-DⓄ́R

▶ **near the exit**

perto da saída

PⒺ̈́R-Tⓞⓞ Dⓐⓗ SⒾ́-ⒺⒺ-Dⓐⓗ

BY BUS

Bus

Ônibus

Ó-NEE-BooS

Where is the bus stop?

Onde fica o ponto de ônibus?

Óñg-JEE FEE-Koo PÓN-Too

JEE Ó-NEE-BooS

Do you go to...?

Você vai para...?

VO-SÁ VI Pah-Rah...

What is the fare?

Quanto é a passagem?

KWahñg-Too ě ah Pah-Sah-ZHAñg

Do I need exact change?

Preciso de troco correto?

PRě-SEE-Zoo JEE TRÓ-Koo

KO-HěB-Too

How often do the buses run?

Com que freqüência passam os ônibus?

KOñg Kě FRě-KWěN-SEEah

PahS-SahM ooS Ó-NEE-BooS

PHRASEMAKER

Please tell me...

Por favor me diga...

POR Fah-VOR ME JEE-Gah...

▸ **which bus goes to...**

que ônibus vai para...

KEE O-NEE-BooS VI Pah-Rah...

▸ **at what time does the bus leave**

a que hora sai o ônibus

ah Kê O-Rah SI oo O-NEE-BooS

▸ **where the bus stop is**

onde fica o ponto de ônibus

ON-JEE FEE-Kah oo PON-Too
JEE O-NEE-BooS

▸ **when we are at...**

quando nós estivermos em...

KWahN-Doo NahS
êS-CHEE-VÔR-MooS êñg...

▸ **where to get off**

onde descer

Oñg-JEE Dê-SêR

BY CAR

Can you help me?

Você pode me ajudar?

V(O)-S(A)´ P(O)´-J(EE) M(EE) (ah)-J(oo)-D(ah)´R

My car won't start.

Meu carro não quer pegar.

M(ĕ)(oo) K(ah)´-H(oo) N(ow)ñg K(ĕ)R P(ĕ)-G(ah)´R

Can you fix it?

Você pode consertá-lo?

V(O)´-S(A) P(O)´-J(EE) K(O)N-S(ĕ)R-T(ah)´-L(oo)

What will it cost?

Quanto vai custar?

KW(ah)´ñg-T(oo) V(I) K(oo)-ST(ah)´R

How long will it take?

Quanto tempo vai demorar?

KW(ah)´ñg-T(oo) T(ĕ)´M-P(oo) V(I) D(ĕ)-M(O)-R(ah)´R

PHRASEMAKER

Please check...

Por favor, verifique...

POR F@h-VOR V@-R@-F@-K@...

▶ **the battery**

a bateria

@h B@h-T@-R@-@h

▶ **the brakes**

os freios

@S FR@-@S

▶ **the oil**

o óleo

@ OL-Y@

▶ **the tires**

os pneus

@S P@-N@-@S

▶ **the water**

a água

@h @h-GW@h

SUBWAYS AND TRAINS

Where is the train station?

Onde fica a estação ferroviária?

Oñg-JEE FEE-Kah ah eS-Tah-Sowñg
Fe-HO-VEE-ahR-EEah

Where is the subway station?

Onde fica a estação de metrô?

Oñg-JEE FEE-Kah ah
eS-Tah-Sowñg JEE Me-TRO

A one-way ticket, please.

Uma passagem de ida por favor.

oo-Mah Pah-Sah-ZHAñg JEE
EE-Dah POR Fah-VOR

A round trip ticket.

Uma passagem de ida e volta.

oo-Mah Pah-Sah-ZHAñg JEE
EE-Dah EE VOL-Tah

First class

Primeira classe

PREE-MA-Rah KLah-SEE

Second class

Segunda classe

Sẽ-G⊚ñg-D⓪ KL⓪S-Sᴇᴇ

What is the fare?

Quanto é a passagem?

KW⓪N-T⊚ ẽ ⓪ P⓪-S⓪-ZH⓪ñg

Is this seat taken?

Este assento está ocupado?

ẽS-CHẽ ⓪S-Sẽñg-T⊚
ẽS-T⓪ ⓪-K⊚-P⓪-D⊚

Do I have to change trains?

Eu tenho que mudar de trem?

ᴇᴇ⊚ Tẽñg-Y⊚ Kẽ
M⊚-D⓪R Jᴇᴇ TRẽñg

Where are we?

Onde estamos?

⊚ñg-Jᴇᴇ ẽS-T⓪-M⊚S

BY TAXI

Please call a taxi for me.

Por favor, me chame um táxi.

POB F@h-V@B M@

SH@h-M@ @@ñg T@hK-S@

Are you available?

Você está livre?

V@-S@ @S-T@h L@V-B@

I want to go to...

Quero ir para...

K@-B@ @B P@h-B@h...

Stop here, please.

Pare aqui, por favor.

P@h-B@ @h-K@ P@B F@h-V@B

Please wait.

Espere por favor.

@S-P@-B@ P@B F@h-V@B

How much do I owe?

Quanto devo?

KW@hN-T@ D@-V@

PHRASEMAKER

I would like to go...

Eu gostaria de ir...

▸ **to this address**

para este endereço

▸ **to the airport**

para o aeroporto

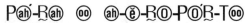

▸ **to the bank**

para o banco

P@h́-R@h ⓞⓞ B@h́N-K⓪⓪

▸ **to the hotel**

para o hotel

P@h́-R@h ⓞⓞ ⓞ-TⓔL

▸ **to the train station**

para a estação ferroviária

Fⓔ-H⓪-VⒺⒺ-@h́R-ⒺⒺ@h

SHOPPING

Whether you plan a major shopping. spree or just need to purchase some basic necessities, the following. information is useful.

- You can find duty-free shops in airports, major train stations, and tourist cities.

- If you go to Rio, the place to buy fruits and vegetables is your neighborhood's street market or "feira." Don't forget that Brazilians use the metric system.

- Major city shops and markets stay open as late as 10:00 p.m.

- There is excellent shopping for clothing found in European sizing 36, 38, 40 etc., or marked pequeno (small), médio (medium) and grande (large).

- You can also find quality leather goods; e.g., belts, purses, shoes and more. Some haggling is acceptable.

- Rio boasts a huge array of beautiful gemstones. Some stores will offer a discount if you pay in cash.

KEY WORDS

Credit card

Cartão de crédito

K(ah)R-T(ów)ñg J(EE) KR(ĕ́)-J(EE)-T(oo)

Money

Dinheiro

J(EE)ñg-Y(ĕ́)-R(oo)

Receipt

Recibo / Nota

H(ĕ)-S(EÉ)-B(oo) / N(ó)-T(ah)

Sale

Venda

V(ĕ́)ñg-D(ah)

Store

Loja

L(ó)-ZH(ah)

Traveler's checks

Cheques de viagem

SH(ĕ́)-K(EE)S J(EE) V(EE)-(áh)-ZH(ĕ)ñg

USEFUL PHRASES

Do you sell...?

Você vende...?

VO-SA VEN-JEE...

Do you have...?

Você tem...?

VO-SA TAñg...

I want to buy.

Eu quero comprar.

EOO KA-ROO KOñg-PRahB

How much?

Quanto?

KWahN-TOO

When does the shop open?

Quando abre a loja?

KWahN-DOO ah-BREñ ah LO-ZHah

When are the shops open?

Quando abrem as lojas?

KWahN-DOO ah-BREñg ahS LO-ZHahS

No, thank you.

Não, obrigado. (m) Não, obrigada. (f)

NⓄWñg Ⓞ-BRⒺⒺ-Gⓐ-DⓄ
NⓄWñg Ⓞ-BRⒺⒺ-Gⓐ-Dⓐ

I'm just looking.

Estou só olhando.

ⒺS-TⓄ SⓄ ⓄL-Yⓐñg-DⓄ

Can you give me a discount?

Pode me dar um desconto?

PⓄ-JⒺⒺ MⒺⒺ Dⓐ R
Ⓞⓞñg JⒺⒺ-SKⓄñg-TⓄ

I'll take it.

Eu levo isto.

Ⓔ Ⓞ LⒺ-VⓄ ⒺⒺS-TⓄ

I'd like a receipt, please.

Eu quero uma nota, por favor.

Ⓔ Ⓞ Kⓐ-RⓄ Ⓞ-Mⓐ NⓄ-Tⓐ
PⓄR Fⓐ-VⓄR

SHOPS AND SERVICES

Bakery
Padaria

P@h-D@h-R@E´-@h

Bank
Banco

B@h´N-K⊚⊚

Hair salon
Cabelereiro

K@h-B@ē-L@ē-R@A´-R⊚⊚

Barbershop
Barbeiro

B@hR-B@A´-R⊚⊚

Jewelry store
Joalheria

ZH⊚@h-L@E-Y@h-R@E´-@h

Bookstore
Livraria

L@EV-R@h-R@E´-@h

News stand
Banca de jornal

B@h´ñg-K@h   J@E
ZH⊚R-N@h´L

Camera shop
Loja de máquinas fotográficas

L⊚´-ZH@h   J@E   M@h´-K@E-N@hS
F⊚-T⊚-GR@h´-F@E-K@hS

Pharmacy
Farmácia

F@hR-M@h´-S@E-@h

SHOPPING LIST

On the following pages you will find some common
items you may need to purchase on your trip.

Aspirin
Aspirina
@S-PEE-REE-N@

Cigarettes
Cigarros
SEE-G@B-H@S

Deodorant
Desodorante
JEE-S@-D@-B@ñg-CHEE

Dress
Vestido
VeS-CHEE-D@

Film
Filme
F@L-MEE

Perfume

Perfume

PⓔR-FⓄⓄ-MⒺⒺ

Razor blades

Giletes

Jⓔ-Lⓔ-TⓔS

Shampoo

Xampu

HⓐⓗM-PⓄⓄ

Shaving cream

Creme de barbear

KRⓔ-MⒺⒺ JⒺⒺ BⓐⓗR-BⒺⒺⓐⓗR

Shirt

Camisa

Kⓐⓗ-MⒺⒺ-Zⓐⓗ

Sunglasses

Óculos de sol

Ⓞ-KⓄⓄ-LⓄⓄS JⒺⒺ SⓄL

Suntan oil

Bronzeador

BRⓐⓗN-ZⒺⒺ-ⓐⓗ-DⓄR

Toothbrushes

Escovas de dentes

ẽS-KŌ'-Vah̃S JEE DẽÑg-CHEES

Toothpaste

Pasta de dentes

Pah̃S-Tah̃ JEE DẽÑg-CHEES

Water (bottled)

Garrafa de água

Gah̃-Hah̃-Fah̃ JEE ah̃'-GWah̃

Water (mineral)

Água mineral

ah̃'-GWah̃ MEE-Nẽ-Ŗow'

ESSENTIAL SERVICES

THE BANK

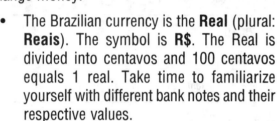

As a traveler in a foreign country your primary contact with banks will be to exchange money.

- The Brazilian currency is the **Real** (plural: **Reais**). The symbol is **R$**. The Real is divided into centavos and 100 centavos equals 1 real. Take time to familiarize yourself with different bank notes and their respective values.

- It is a good idea to hold on to small bills R$1 or R$5s because street vendors, shops, etc., can not always make change for higher currency bills. You may have to wait or come back later.

- Currency exchange businesses exist in all major cities. "Casas de Câmbio" are establishments that deal only with currencies. When changing US dollars for Reals, keep your receipt in case you want to change back from reals to dollars.

- Most major credit cards are accepted; however, it is a good idea to check with your bank to see if yours is accepted. Transactions are limited.

KEY WORDS

Bank

Banco

B@h'N-K@@

Exchange office

Casa de câmbio

K@h'-Z@h J@@ K@h'ñg-B@@-@@

Money

Dinheiro

D@@ñg-Y@'-R@@

Money order

Vale postal

V@h'-L@@ P@@S-T@h'L

Traveler's check

Cheque de viagem

SH@'-K@@ D@@ V@@-@h'-ZH@'ñg

Brazilian Currency

Real (sg)	Reais (pl)	Centavos
H@'-@h'L	H@'-@'S	S@'N-T@h'-V@@S

Note: Travelers checks are difficult to use in Brazil. Exchange rates are high and many shops do not accept them. It is a good idea to have US dollars to use in emergencies.

USEFUL PHRASES

Where is the bank?

Onde fica o banco?

Oñg-JEE FEE-Kah oo BahN-Koo

What time does the bank open?

A que horas o banco abre?

ah KA O-RahS oo
BahN-Koo ah-BREE

Where is the exchange office?

Onde fica a casa de câmbio?

ON-JEE FEE-Kah ah Kah-Zah
JEE KahM-BEE-oo

What time does the exchange office open?

A que horas a casa de câmbio abre?

ah KA O-RahS ah Kah-Zah JEE
KahM-BEE-oo ah-BREE

Can I change dollars here?

Posso trocar dólares aqui?

POS-Soo TRO-KahB
DO-Lah-RëS ah-KEE

What is the exchange rate?

Qual é a taxa de câmbio?

QWahL ê ah Tah-SHah
JEE KahM-BEE-oo

I would like large bills.

Eu quero notas grandes.

êoo Kê-Roo
NOO-TahS GRahN-JEES

I would like small bills.

Eu quero notas pequenas.

êoo Kê-Roo
NOO-TahS Pê-Kê-N-ahS

I need change.

Eu preciso de troco.

êoo PRê-SEE-Zoo
JEE TROO-Koo

Do you have an ATM?

Tem caixa eletrônico?

TAñg KI-ZHah
EE-Lê-TROON-EE-Koo

POST OFFICE

If you are planning on sending letters and postcards, be sure to send them early so that you don't arrive home before they do.

KEY WORDS

Air mail

Por avião

PⓄⓇ ⓐⓗ-Vⓔⓔ-ⓄⓌñg

Letter

Carta

KⓐⓇ-Tⓐⓗ

Note: Addresses in Brazil are written with the street name first, followed by the street number.

Post office

Correio

KⓄ-Hⓐ-ⓄⓄ

Postcard

Cartão postal

KⓐⓇ-TⓄⓌñg PⓄS-TⓐⓗL

Stamp

Selo

Sⓔ-LⓄⓄ

USEFUL PHRASES

Where is the post office?

Onde é o correio?

Oñg-JEE ě oo KO-HA´-oo

What time does the post office open?

A que horas o correio abre?

ah KA O´-RahS oo
KO-HA´-oo ah-BREE

I need...

Eu preciso...

ěoo PRě-SEE´-Zoo...

I need stamps.

Preciso de selos.

PRě-SEE´-Zoo JEE Sě-LooS

I need an envelope.

Preciso de um envelope.

PRě-SEE´-Zoo JEE ooñg EEN-Vě-LSO´-PEE

I need a pen.

Preciso de uma caneta.

PREE-SEE´-Zoo JEE oo´-Mah Kah-Ně-Tah

TELEPHONE

Placing phone calls in Brazil can be
a test of will and stamina! Besides
the obvious language barriers, service
can vary greatly from one town to the
next.

- There are three time zones in Brazil!

- Public telephones "orelhões" are located
  everywhere. You need telephone cards
  called "cartão telefônico" to use them.
  Phone cards can be purchased at news
  stands.

- In your hotel you can use your international
  calling card as long as you have the access
  number to dial the operator. This is usually
  cheaper.

- Internet service is widely available and
  larger hotels offer high-speed internet
  service and will charge per hour.

- Internet services found in internet cafes
  will usually be less expensive.

KEY WORDS

Information

Informação

ⒺN-FⓄB-Mⓐ-Sⓞⓦñg

Long distance

Ligação interurbana

Lⓔ-Gⓐ-Sⓞⓦñg ⒺN-Tⓔ-Bⓞⓞ-Bⓐ-Nⓐ

Operator

Telefonista

Tⓔ-Lⓔ-FⓄ-Nⓔ-STⓐ

Phone book

Lista telefônica

Lⓔ'S-Tⓐ Tⓔ-Lⓔ-FⓄ-Nⓔ-Kⓐ

Public telephone

Telefone público

Tⓔ-Lⓔ-FⓄ-Nⓔ PⓞⓞB-Lⓔ-Kⓞⓞ

USEFUL PHRASES

Where is the telephone?

Onde é o telefone?

Oñg-JEE   é   oo   Tĕh-Lĕh-FO-NEE

Where is the public telephone?

Onde é o telefone público?

Oñg-JEE   é   oo   Tĕh-Lĕh-FO-NEE
Poo-B-LEE-Koo

May I use your telephone?

Posso usar o seu telefone?

PO-S-Soo   oo-SahR   oo   Sĕh-oo
Tĕh-Lĕh-FO-NEE

Operator, I don't speak Portuguese.

Telefonista, eu não falo português.

Tĕh-Lĕh-FO-NEE-STah   ĕh-oo   Nowñg
Fah-Loo   POR-Too-Gĕh-S

I would like to make a long distance call.

Quero fazer uma ligação interurbana.

Kĕh-Roo   Fah-ZĕhR   oo-Mah
LEE-Gah-Sowñg   EEN-Tĕh-Roo-Bah-Nah

I want to call this number...

Quero ligar para este número...

Kẽ-Ŕoo Lĕɛ-Gah̓Ŕ PŔah ĕS-CHɛɛ
Noo-Mẽ-Ŕoo...

1 um oõ̃g	**2** dois Doy̓S	**3** três TŔẽS
4 quatro QWah̓-TŔoo	**5** cinco SɛɛN-Koo	**6** seis Sa̓S
7 sete Sẽ-CHɛɛ	**8** oito oy̓-Too	**9** nove Noó-Vɛɛ
$\ast$	**0** zero Zẽ-Ŕoo	**#**

SIGHTSEEING AND ENTERTAINMENT

Brasília is the country's capital and Portuguese is the official language. English is spoken widely. Important sights include Iguaçu Falls, the Amazon, Salvador and Recife. São Paulo is South America's largest city and is Brazil's center of trade and industry.

RIO DE JANEIRO BRAZIL

Rio de Janeiro is truly a "cidade maravilhosa," spectacularly located. Corcovado - Christ the Redeemer statue has become a universal symbol of a city that welcomes its visitors with open arms.

Another famous land-mark is Sugar Loaf Mountain where you will enjoy a magnificent view of the city, sea and mountains.

KEY WORDS

Admission

Entrada

ĕñg-TRah́-Dah

Map

Mapa

Mah́-Pah

Reservation

Reserva

Hĕ̃-SĕR-Vah

Ticket

Entrada / Bilhete

ĕñg-TRah́-Dah / BEEL-Yĕ̃-CHEE

Tour

Passeio

Pah̃S-Sah́-Yoo

Tour guide

Guia turístico

GEÉah Too-REÉS-CHEE-Koo

USEFUL PHRASES

Where is the tourist agency?

Onde fica a agência de turismo?

Ong-JEE FEE-Kah

A-ZHAng-SEE-ah JEE TOO-REES-Moo

Where do I buy a ticket?

Onde eu compro uma passagem?

Ong-JEE EE-oo KOM-PRoo oo-Mah

Pah-Sah-ZHEng

Is there a tour to...?

Tem uma excursão para...?

TAng oo-Mah eS-KooR-Song Pah-Rah...

How much does the tour cost?

Quanto custa a excursão?

KWahng-Too KooS-Tah ah

eS-KooR-Song

How long does the tour take?

Quanto tempo dura a excursão?

KWahng-Too TeM-Poo Doo-Rah

eS-KooR-Song

Does the guide speak English?

O guia fala inglês?

ⓞ Gⓔⓔ-ⓐⓗ Fⓐⓗ-Lⓐⓗ ⓔⓔñg-GLⓔ́S

How much do children pay?

Quanto pagam as crianças?

KWⓐⓗñg-Tⓞⓞ Pⓐⓗ-Gⓐⓗñg ⓐⓗS
KRⓔⓔ-ⓐⓗñg-SⓐⓗS

What time does the show start?

A que hora começa o espetáculo?

ⓐⓗ Kⓔⓔ ⓞ-Rⓐⓗ Kⓞ-Mⓔ́-Sⓐⓗⓞⓞ
ⓔⓔS-Pⓔ́-Tⓐ́-Kⓞⓞ-Lⓞⓞ

Do I need reservations?

Preciso de reserva?

PRⓔ́-Sⓔⓔ-Zⓞⓞ Jⓔⓔ Hⓔ́-Sⓔ́R-Vⓐⓗ

Where can we go dancing?

Onde podemos ir dançar?

Ⓞ́ñg-Jⓔⓔ Pⓞ-Dⓔ́-MⓞⓞS
ⓔⓔR DⓐⓗN-Sⓐⓗ́R

Is there a minimum cover charge?

Tem couvert? / Tem consumo mínimo?

Tⓔ́ñg Kⓞⓞ-Vⓔ́R
Tⓔ́ñg KⓞN-Sⓞⓞ́-Mⓞⓞ Mⓔⓔ́-Nⓔⓔ-Mⓞⓞ

PHRASEMAKER

May I invite you...

Posso te convidar...

PⓄS-Sⓞⓞ   CHⒺⒺ   KⓄN-VⒺⒺ-DⓐⓗʼR...

▸ **to a concert?**

para um concerto?

Pⓐⓗʼ-Rⓐⓗ   ⓞⓞñg   KⓄN-SⒺʼⓡⓇ-Tⓞⓞ

▸ **to a dance?**

para dançar?

Pⓐⓗʼ-Rⓐⓗ   DⓐⓗN-SⓐⓗʼR

▸ **to dinner?**

para um jantar?

Pⓐⓗʼ-Rⓐⓗ   ⓞⓞñg   ZHⓐⓗN-TⓐⓗʼR

▸ **to the movies?**

para ir ao cinema?

Pⓐⓗʼ-Rⓐⓗ   ⒺⒺR   ⓄWñg   SⒺⒺN-Ⓐʼ-Mⓐⓗ

▸ **to the theater?**

para ir ao teatro?

Pⓐⓗʼ-Rⓐⓗ   ⒺⒺR   ⓄWñg   TⒺⒺ-ⓐⓗʼ-TRⓞⓞ

PHRASEMAKER

Where can I find...

Onde posso encontrar...

Oñg-JⒺ PⓄS-Sⓞ ⓔN-KⓄN-TRⓐR...

▶ **a health club**

uma academia

ⓞ-Mⓐ Kⓐ-Dⓔ-MⒺ-ⓐ

▶ **a swimming pool**

uma piscina

ⓞ-Mⓐ PⒺ-SⒺ-Nⓐ

▶ **a tennis court**

uma quadra de tênis

ⓞ-Mⓐ KWⓐ-DRⓐ JⒺ Tⓔ-NⒺS

▶ **a golf course**

um campo de golfe

ⓞñg KⓐM-Pⓞ JⒺ GⓄL-FⒺ

HEALTH

Hopefully you will not need medical attention on your trip. If you do, it is important to communicate basic information regarding your condition.

- Check with your insurance company before leaving home to find out if you are covered in a foreign country. You may want to purchase traveler's insurance before leaving home.

- If you take prescription medicine, carry your prescription with you.

- Take a small first-aid kit with you. You may want to include basic cold and anti-diarrhea medications. However, you should be able to find most items like aspirin locally.

- It is a good idea to drink only bottled or filtered water. It is not advisable to eat from vendors in the street.

- If you do end up with a stomach upset and need to visit the pharmacy, there is usually a licensed pharmacist trained to help in small medical emergencies.

KEY WORDS

Ambulance

Ambulância

ah-M-Boo-L-ah-ñg-SEE-ah

Dentist

Dentista

DeN-CH-EE-S-Tah

Doctor

Médico (m)   Médica (f)

Me-JEE-Koo   (ah)

Emergency

Emergência

e-Me-R-ZH-e-ñg-SEE-ah

Hospital

Hospital

OS-P-EE-Tah-L

Prescription

Receita

He-SA-Tah

USEFUL PHRASES

I am sick.

Estou doente.

ⒺS-TⓄ DⓄ-ⓔñg-CHⒺ

I need a doctor.

Preciso de um médico.

PRⓔ-SⒺ-Zⓞⓞ JⒺ ⓞⓞñg

Mⓔ-JⒺ-Kⓞⓞ

It's an emergency!

Isto é uma emergência!

ⒺS-Tⓞⓞ ⓔ ⓞⓞ-Mⓐⓗ

ⓔ-MⓔR-ZHⓔñg-SⒺ-ⓐⓗ

Where is the nearest hospital?

Onde fica o hospital mais perto?

Ⓞñg-JⒺ FⒺ-Kⓐⓗ ⓞⓞ

ⓄS-PⒺ-TⓐⓗL MⒾS PⓔR-Tⓞⓞ

Call an ambulance!

Chame uma ambulância!

SHⓐⓗ-MⒺ ⓞⓞ-Mⓐⓗ

ⓐⓗM-Bⓞⓞ-Lⓐⓗñg-SⒺ-ⓐⓗ

I'm allergic to...

Eu sou alérgico a... (m)

ⓔⓞⓞ Sⓞ ⓐⓗ-LⓔⓡR-ZHⒺⒺ-Kⓞⓞ ⓐⓗ...

I'm allergic to...

Eu sou alérgica a... (f)

ⓔⓞⓞ Sⓞ ⓐⓗ-LⓔⓡR-ZHⒺⒺ-Kⓐⓗ ⓐⓗ...

I'm pregnant.

Estou grávida.

ⒺⒺS-Tⓞ GRⓐⓗ-VⒺⒺ-Dⓐⓗ

I'm diabetic.

Sou diabético. (m)   Sou diabética. (f)

Sⓞ JⒺⒺⓐⓗ-Bⓔⓡ-CHⒺⒺ-Kⓞⓞ (ⓐⓗ)

I have a heart condition.

Eu sofro do coração.

ⓔⓞⓞ Sⓞⓡ-FRⓞⓞ Dⓞⓞ Kⓞ-Rⓐⓗ-Sⓞⓦñg

I have high blood pressure.

Eu tenho pressão alta.

ⓔⓞⓞ Tⓔⓡñg-Yⓞⓞ PRⓔS-Sⓞⓦñg ⓐⓗL-Tⓐⓗ

I have low blood pressure.

Eu tenho pressão baixa.

ⓔⓞⓞ Tⓔⓡñg-Yⓞⓞ PRⓔS-Sⓞⓦñg Bⓘ-SHⓐⓗ

PHRASEMAKER

I need...

Eu preciso...

ⓔ⊚ PRⓔ-Sⓔ́Ē-Z⊚...

▶ **a doctor**

de um médico (m)
de uma médica (f)

Jⓔ ⊚ñg Mⓔ-Jⓔ-K⊚

Jⓔ ⊚́-Mⓐ Mⓔ-Jⓔ-Kⓐ

▶ **a dentist**

de um dentista

Jⓔ ⊚ñg Dⓔ̃ñg-Tⓔ́S-Tⓐ

▶ **a nurse**

de um enfermeiro (m)
de uma enfermeira (f)

Jⓔ ⊚ñg ⓔN-Fⓔ̃R-MⒶ́-R⊚

Jⓔ ⊚́-Mⓐ ⓔN-Fⓔ̃R-MⒶ́-Rⓐ

▶ **a pharmacist**

de um farmacêutico (m)
de uma farmacêutica (f)

Jⓔ ⊚ñg FⓐR-Mⓐ-Sⓔ̃⊚-CHⓔ-K⊚

Jⓔ ⊚́-Mⓐ FⓐR-Mⓐ-Sⓔ̃⊚-CHⓔ-Kⓐ

PHRASEMAKER
(AT THE PHARMACY)

Do you have...

Você tem...

VO͞-SA͞   TA͞ñg...

▸ **aspirin?**

aspirina?

ahS-PEE-REE-Nah

▸ **Band-Aids?**

Band Aid / esparadrapo?

BahN-DA-JEE / ĕS-Pah-Rah-DRah-Poo

▸ **cough syrup?**

xarope para tosse?

SHah-RO-PEE Pah-Rah TOS-SEE

▸ **ear drops?**

gotas para o ouvido?

GO-TahS Pah-Rah oo O-VEE-Doo

▸ **eye drops?**

colírio?

KO-LEE-REEoo

BUSINESS TRAVEL

It is important to show appreciation and interest in another person's language and culture, particularly when doing business. A few well-pronounced phrases can make a great impression.

- Exchanging business cards is very important, so be sure to bring a good supply with you.

- Doing business is a type of social interaction in Brazil. People need to get acquainted and comfortable with each other before getting down to business.

- Executive dress is defined by three-piece suit attire, while general office or employees are defined by a two-piece suit.

- Business dress is conservative for woman and well groomed nails are very important.

- Do not use the OK hand signal as it is considered a rude gesture.

- Do not wear yellow and green combination colors as these are the colors of the Brazilian flag.

- Shake hands at greeting and leaving.

- First names can be used; however, titles are important.

KEY WORDS

Appointment
Hora marcada

Ⓞ-Ⓡ@h M@hⓇ-Ⓚ@h-Ⓓ@h

Business card
Cartão de visita

Ⓚ@hⓇ-Tⓞwñg J㉫ Vㅌㅌ-Sㅌㅌ-T@h

Meeting
Reunião

Hㅔ-ⓞⓞ-Nㅌㅌ-ⓞwñg

Marketing
Marketing

M@hⓇ-Ⓚㅔ-CHㅌㅌñg

Office
Escritório

ㅔ-SKⓇㅌㅌ-TⓞⓇ-ㅌㅌ-ⓞⓞ

Presentation
Apresentação

@h-PⓇㅔ-Zㅔñg-T@h-Sⓞwñg

Telephone
Telefone

Tㅔ-Lㅔ-Fⓞ-Nㅌㅌ

USEFUL PHRASES

I have an appointment.

Eu tenho uma hora marcada.

ⓔ⓪⓪ Tⓔñg-Y⓪⓪ ⓞⓞ-Mⓐⓗ
Ⓞ-Ⓡⓐⓗ MⓐⓗⓇ-Kⓐⓗ-Dⓐⓗ

My name is...(your name).

Meu nome é…(your name).

Mⓔⓔ⓪⓪ NⓄ-MⓔⒺ ⓔ…(your name)

Pleased to meet you.

Prazer em conhecê-lo. (m)
Prazer em conhecê-la. (f)

PⓇⓐⓗ-ZⓔⓇ Ⓐñg KⓄN-Yⓔ-SⒶ-L⓪⓪
PⓇⓐⓗ-ZⓔⓇ Ⓐñg KⓄN-Yⓔ-SⒶ-Lⓐⓗ

Here is my card.

Aqui está o meu cartão.

ⓐⓗ-KⒺⒺ ⓔS-Tⓐⓗ ⓞⓞ
Mⓔⓔ⓪⓪ KⓐⓗⓇ-T⓪ⓦñg

Can we get an interpreter?

Podemos ter um intérprete?

P⓪-Dⓔ-M⓪⓪S TⓔⓇ ⓞⓞñg
ⒺⒺñg-TⓔⓇ-PⓇⓔ-CHⒺⒺ

Can you write your address for me?

Você pode escrever o seu endereço?

VO-SA PAH-JEE ES-KREE-VER
OO SEE00 EN-DER-SOO

Can you write your phone number?

Você pode escrever o seu número de telefone?

VO-SA PAH-JEE OO SEE00
ES-KREE-VER NOO-MEE-ROO
JEE TEE-LEE-FO-NEE

This is my phone number.

Este é o meu número de telefone.

ES-CHEE EE OO MEE00
NOO-MEE-ROO JEE TEE-LEE-FO-NEE

His name is...

O nome dele é...

OO NO-MEE DEE-LEE EE...

Her name is...

O nome dela é...

OO NO-MEE DEE-LAH EE

Good-bye.
Tchau.

CHOW

PHRASEMAKER

I need...

Eu preciso...

ẽoo PRẽ-SEE-Zoo...

▶ **a computer**

de um computador

JEE ooñg KOM-Poo-Tah-DOB

▶ **a copy machine**

de um xerox

JEE ooñg SHẽ-BOKS

▶ **a conference room**

de uma sala de reunião

JEE oo-Mah Sah-Lah JEE
Hẽoo-NEEowñg

▶ **a fax or fax machine**

de um fax

JEE ooñg FahKS

▶ **an interpreter**

de um intérprete

JEE ooñg EEñg-TẽB-PRẽ-CHEE

▶ **a lawyer**

de um advogado (m) de um advogada (f)

JÊ ooñg ah-JEE-VO-Gah-Doo (ah)

▶ **a notary**

de um notário (m) de um notária (f)

JEE ooñg NO-Tah'R-EEoo (ah)

▶ **a pen**

de uma caneta

JEE oo'-Mah Kah-NÊ'-Tah

▶ **stamps**

de selos

JEE SÊ'-LooS

▶ **stationery**

de papel de carta

JEE Pah-PÊ'L JEE Kah'R-Tah

▶ **typing paper**

de papel para datilografar

JEE Pah-PÊ'L Pah'-Rah
Dah-CHEE-LO-GRah-Fah'R

GENERAL INFORMATION

Brazil has five climatic regions. São Paulo and Brasília have a mild climate while Rio de Janeiro, Recife, Natal and Salvador enjoy warmer climates tempered by tradewinds.

SEASONS

Spring

Primavera

PREE-Mah-VĕR-Rah

Summer

Verão

Vĕ-Rowñg

Autumn

Outono

O-TO-Noo

Winter

Inverno

EEñg-VĕR-Noo

THE DAYS

Monday

segunda-feira

Së-Goong-Dah FÁ-Rah

Tuesday

terça-feira

Tëʀ-Sah FÁ-Rah

Wednesday

quarta-feira

KWahʀ-Tah FÁ-Rah

Thursday

quinta-feira

Keen-Tah FÁ-Rah

Friday

sexta-feira

Sës-Tah FÁ-Rah

Saturday

sábado

Sah-Bah-Doo

Sunday

domingo

Do-Meen-Goo

THE MONTHS

January

janeiro

ZH(ah)-N(A)́-R(oo)

February

fevereiro

F(ẽ)-V(ẽ)-R(A)́-R(oo)

March

março

M(ah)́R-S(oo)

April

abril

(ah)-BR(EE)́L

May

maio

M(ah)́-Y(oo)

June

junho

ZH(oo)́ñg-Y(oo)

July

julho

ZH(oo)́L-Y(oo)

August

agosto

(ah)-G(O)́S-T(oo)

September

setembro

S(ẽ)-T(ẽ)́ñg-BR(oo)

October

outubro

(O)-T(oo)́-BR(oo)

November

novembro

N(O)-V(ẽ)́M-BR(oo)

December

dezembro

D(ẽ)-Z(ẽ)́M-BR(oo)

COLORS

Black
preto (m) Preta (f)
PRĔ-T⊚ (ⓐⓗ)

White
branco (m) branca (f)
BRⓐⓗñg-K⊚ (ⓐⓗ)

Blue
azul
ⓐⓗ-Z⊚́L

Brown
marrom
Mⓐⓗ-HŌñg

Gray
cinza
SEÉ̃ñg-Zⓐⓗ

Gold
dourado (m) dourada (f)
DŌ-Rⓐⓗ́-D⊚ (ⓐⓗ)

Orange
laranja
Lⓐⓗ-Rⓐ̃ñg-ZHⓐⓗ

Yellow
amarelo (m) amarela (f)
ⓐⓗ-Mⓐ̃-RĔ-L⊚ (ⓐⓗ)

Red
vermelho (m) vermelha (f)
VĔR-MĔL-Y⊚ (ⓐⓗ)

Green
verde
VĔR-JEE

Pink
rosa
HṒ-Zⓐⓗ

Purple
roxo (m) roxa (f)
HṒ-SH⊚ (ⓐⓗ)

NUMBERS

0	1	2
Zero	Um	Dois
Zĕ́-Roo	oṍñg	Dọ̄S

3	4	5
Três	Quatro	Cinco
TRĕ̃S	KWah́-TRoo	SEÉN-Koo

6	7	8
Seis	Sete	Oito
SⒶS	Sĕ́-CHEE	oỳ-Too

9	10	11
Nove	Dez	Onze
Nó-VEE	Dĕ̃Z	Óñg-ZEE

12	13	14
Doze	Treze	Quatorze
Doó-ZEE	TRĕ̃-ZEE	Kah́-TOŕ-ZEE

15	16
Quinze	Dezesseis
KEEÑg-ZEE	Dĕ̃-Zĕ́-SⒶS

17	18
Dezessete	Dezoito
Dĕ̃-Sĕ̃-Sĕ́-CHEE	Dĕ̃-Zoỳ-Too

19	**20**
Dezenove	Vinte
Dĕ-Zĕ-NŌ-VEE	VEEN-CHEE

30	**40**
Trinta	Quarenta
TREEN-Tah	KWah-RĕN-Tah

50	**60**
Cinqüenta	Sessenta
SEEñg-KWĕN-Tah	SĕS-SĕN-Tah

70	**80**
Setenta	Oitenta
Sĕ-TĕN-Tah	oy-TĕN-Tah

90	**100**
Noventa	Cem
NŌ-VĕN-Tah	SAM

1,000	**1,000,000**
Mil	Um milhão
MEEL	ooñg MEE-LEE-owñg

DICTIONARY

Each English entry is followed
by the Portuguese word and
then the EPLS Vowel Symbol
System. Masculine words will
be indicated by (m), and feminine
by (f). Singular will be indicated by
(s) and plural by (pl) respectively.

A ⓞⓦ ñg ①

a, an um (m) uma (f) ⓞⓞñg / ⓞⓞ-Mⓐ

a lot muito MWⓔñg-Tⓞⓞ

able capaz Kⓐ-PⓐZ

accident acidente ⓐ-Sⓔ-Dⓔñg-CHⓔ

accommodation acomodação ⓐ-Kⓞ-Mⓞ-Dⓐ-Sⓞⓦñg

account conta KⓞN-Tⓐ

address endereço ⓔñg-Dⓔ-Rⓔ-Sⓞⓞ

admission entrada ⓔñg-TBⓐ-Dⓐ

afraid receoso (m) receosa (f)
Hⓔ-Sⓔ-ⓞ-Zⓞⓞ / Hⓔ-Sⓔ-ⓞ-Zⓐ

after depois Dⓔ-PⓞⓨS

afternoon tarde TⓐB-Jⓔ

agency agência ⓐ-ZHⓔñg-Sⓔ-ⓐ

air-conditioning ar condicionado
ⓐR Kⓞñg-Dⓔ-Sⓔ-ⓞⓞN-ⓐ-Dⓞⓞ

aircraft avião ⓐ-Vⓔ-ⓞⓦñg

airline linha aérea LEEN-Yah ah-EE-REE-ah

airport aeroporto ah-EE-RO-POR-Too

aisle corredor KO-HEE-DOR

all todos (m,pl) todas (f,pl) TO-DooS / TO-DahS

all (everything) tudo Too-Doo

almost quase KWah-ZEE

alone sozinho (m) sozinha (f) SO-ZEEñg-Yoo (ah)

also também Tahñg-BEEñg

always sempre SEEñg-PREE

ambulance ambulância ahM-Boo-Lahñg-SEE-ah

American americano (m) americana (f)
ah-MEE-REE-Kah-Noo / ah-MEE-REE-Kah-Nah

and e EE

another outro (m) outra (f) O-TRoo / O-TRah

anything qualquer coisa KWah L-KER Koy-Zah

apartment apartamento ah-PahR-Tah-MEEN-Too

appetizers aperitivos ah-PEE-REE-CHEE-VooS

apple maçã Mah-Sahñg

appointment hora marcada O-Rah MahR-Kah-Dah

April abril ah-BREEL

arrival chegada SHEE-Gah-Dah

ashtray cinzeiro SEEñg-ZA-Roo

aspirin aspirina ahS-PEE-REE-Nah

attention　atenção　ⓐⓗ-TⓔN-Sⓞⓦñg

August　agosto　ⓐⓗ-GⓄS-Tⓞⓞ

Australia　Austrália　ⓞⓦS-TⓇⓐⓗ-LⓔⒺⓐⓗ

Australian　australiano (m)　australiana (f)
　　ⓞⓦS-TⓇⓐⓗ-LⓔⒺⓐⓗ-Nⓞⓞ　/　ⓞⓦS-TⓇⓐⓗ-LⓔⒺⓐⓗ-Nⓐⓗ

author　autor　ⓞⓦ-TⓄB

automobile　carro　Kⓐⓗ-Hⓞⓞ

autumn　outono　Ⓞ-TⓄ-Nⓞⓞ

avenue　avenida　ⓐⓗ-Vⓔ-NⒺⒺ-Dⓐⓗ

awful　terrível　Tⓔ-HⒺⒺ-VⓔL

B

baby　bebê　Bⓔ-Bⓔ

babysitter　babá　Bⓐⓗ-Bⓐⓗ

bacon　bacon　BⒶ-KⓄñg

bad　mau / má　Mⓞⓦ / Mⓐⓗ

bag　mala　Mⓐⓗ-Lⓐⓗ

baggage　bagagem　Bⓐⓗ-Gⓐⓗ-ZHⓔñg

baked　assado (m)　assada (f)　ⓐⓗ-Sⓐⓗ-Dⓞⓞ　(ⓐⓗ)

bakery　padaria　Pⓐⓗ-Dⓐⓗ-RⒺⒺ-ⓐⓗ

banana　banana　Bⓐⓗ-Nⓐⓗ-Nⓐⓗ

Band-Aid　Band Aid / esparadrapo
　　BⓐⓗN-DⒶ-JⒺⒺ　/　ⓔS-Pⓐⓗ-Rⓐⓗ-DRⓐⓗ-Pⓞⓞ

bank　banco　BⓐⓗN-Kⓞⓞ

barber barbeiro B@B-B@-R@

bartender garçom G@B-SOñg

bath banho B@ñg-Y@

bathing suit maiô M①-Y①

bathroom banheiro B@N-Y@-R@

battery (car) bateria B@-T@-R@-@

beach praia PB①-Y@

beautiful lindo (m) linda (f)
L@N-D@ / L@N-D@

beauty shop salão de beleza
S@-L@ñg J@ B@-L@-Z@

bed cama K@-M@

beef carne de vaca K@B-N@ J@ V@-K@

beer cerveja S@B-V@-ZH@

bellman carregador K@-H@-G@-D@B

belt cinto S@ñg-T@

big grande GB@ñg-J@

bill conta K①ñg-T@

black preto (m) preta (f) PB@-T@ (@)

blanket cobertor K①-B@B-T①B

blue azul @-Z@L

boat barco B@B-K@

book livro L@V-R@

bookstore   livraria   LEE-VRah-REE-ah

border   fronteira   FROñg-TA'-Rah

boy   menino   ME-NEE-Noo

bracelet   pulseira   POOL-SA'-Rah

brakes   freios   FRA-ooS

bread   pão   Powñg

breakfast   café da manhã   Kah-FE' DA MAHñg-Yah'

broiled   grelhado (m) grelhada (f)
   GRE'L-Yah-Doo / GRE'L-Yah-Dah

brother   irmão   EER-Mowñg

brown   marrom   Mah-HOñg

brush   escova   E'S-KO-Vah

building   edifício   E'-JEE-FEE-SEE-oo

bus   ônibus   O'-NEE-BooS

bus station   estação rodoviária
   EES-Tah-Sowñg HO-DO-VEE-ah'-REE-ah

bus stop   ponto de ônibus
   PO'ñg-Too JEE O'-NEE-BooS

business   negócios   NE-GO'-SEE-ooS

butter   manteiga   MahN-TA'-Gah

buy (to)   comprar   KO'M-PRah'R

C

cab   táxi   Tah'K-SEE

call ligação telefoneca
LEE-Gah-Sowng TEE-LEE-FOO-NEE-Kah

camera câmara Kah-Mah-Rah

Canada Canadá Kah-Nah-Dah

Canadian canadense Kah-Nah-DEEng-SEE

candy (hard candy) balas Bah-Lah S

candy (sweets) doce DOO-SEE

car carro Kah-Hoo

carrot cenoura SEE-NOO-Rah

castle castelo KahS-TEE-Loo

cathedral catedral Kah-TEE-DRowL

celebration comemoração KOO-MEE-MOR-ah-Sowng

center centro SEN-TRoo

cereal cereal SEE-REE-owL

chair cadeira Kah-DA-Rah

champagne champanhe SHahM-Pahng-YEE

change (to) mudar / trocar Moo-DahR / TROO-KahR

change (money) troco TROO-Koo

cheap barato (m) / barata (f)
Bah-Rah-Too / Bah-Rah-Tah

check (restaurant bill) conta KOOng-Tah

cheers! saúde Sahoo-JEE

cheese queijo KA-ZHoo

chicken　frango　FR@ñg-G@

child　criança　KR@-@ñg-S@

chocolate　chocolate　SH@-K@-L@-CH@

church　igreja　@-GR@-ZH@

cigar　charuto　SH@-R@-T@

cigarette　cigarro　S@-G@-H@

city　cidade　S@-D@-J@

clean　limpo (m) limpa (f)　L@ñg-P@　(@)

close (to)　fechar　F@-SH@R

closed　fechado (m) fechada (f)　F@-SH@-D@　(@)

clothes　roupas　H@-P@S

cocktail　coquetel　K@-K@-T@L

coffee　café　K@-F@

cold (temperature)　frio (m) fria (f)
　FR@-@ / FR@-@

comb　pente　P@ñg-CH@

come (here)　vem　V@ñg

company　companhia　K@ñg-P@-N@-Y@

computer　computador　K@ñg-P@-T@-D@R

concert　concerto　K@N-S@R-T@

condom　camisinha　K@-M@-Z@N-Y@

conference　conferência / reunião
　K@N-F@R-@N-S@@ / H@-@-N@-@ñg

conference room sala de reunião
SAH-LAH JEE HAOO-NEE-OWñg

congratulations felicidades FEH-LEE-SEE-DAH-JEES

contraceptive anti concepcional
AHN-TEE KON-SEP-SNAHL

copy machine (xerox) copiadora KO-PEE-AH-DOR-AH

corn milho MEEL-YOO

cough medicine xarope para tosse
SHAH-ROO-PEE PAH-RAH TOS-SEE

cover charge couvert KOO-VEHR

crab caranguejo KAH-RAHñg-GEH-ZHOO

cream creme KREH-MEE

credit card cartão de crédito
KAHR-TOWñg JEE KREH-JEE-TOO

cup xícara SHEE-KAH-RAH

customs alfândega AHL-FAHN-JEE-GAH

D

dance (to) dança DAHñg-SAH

dangerous perigoso (m) perigosa (f)
PEH-REE-GO-ZOO / PEH-REE-GO-ZAH

date (calender) data DAH-TAH

day dia JEE-AH

December dezembro DEH-ZEHM-BROO

delicious delicioso (m) deliciosa (f)
  DⒺ-LⒺS-YⓄ-Zⓞⓞ / DⒺ-LⒺS-YⓄ-Zⓐⓗ

delighted encantado (m) encantada (f)
  ⒺN-KⓐⓗN-Tⓐⓗ-Dⓞⓞ / ⒺN-KⓐⓗN-Tⓐⓗ-Dⓐⓗ

dentist dentista DⒺñg-TⒺ-STⓐⓗ

deodorant desodorante JⒺ-ZⓄ-DⓄ-Bⓐñg-CHⒺ

department store loja de departamentos
  LⓄ-ZHⓐⓗ JⒺ DⒺ-PⓐⓗR-TⒺ-MⒺN-TⓄS

departure partida PⓐⓗR-CHⒺ-Dⓐⓗ

dessert sobremesa SⓄ-BBⒺ-MⒺ-Zⓐⓗ

detour desvio DⒺS-VⒺ-ⓞⓞ

diabetic diabético (m) diabética (f)
  JⒺⓐⓗ-BⒺ-CHⒺ-Kⓞⓞ / JⒺ-ⓐⓗ-BⒺ-CHⒺ-Kⓐⓗ

diarrhea diarréia JⒺ-ⓐⓗ-BⒶ-ⓐⓗ

dictionary dicionário JⒺ-SⒺⓄ-Nⓐⓗ-BⒺⓞⓞ

dinner jantar ZHⓐⓗñg-TⓐⓗB

dining room sala de jantar
  Sⓐⓗ-Lⓐⓗ JⒺ ZHⓐⓗñg-TⓐⓗB

direction direção DⒺ-BⒺ-Sⓞⓦñg

dirty sujo (m) suja (f) Sⓞⓞ-ZHⓞⓞ / Sⓞⓞ-ZHⓐⓗ

disabled incapacitado (m) incapacitada (f)
  ⒺN-Kⓐⓗ-Pⓐⓗ-SⒺ-Tⓐⓗ-Dⓞⓞ / ⒺN-Kⓐⓗ-Pⓐⓗ-SⒺ-Tⓐⓗ-Dⓐⓗ

discount desconto JⒺS-KⓄñg-Tⓞⓞ

distance distância JⒺS-TⓐⓗN-SⒺ-ⓐⓗ

doctor médico (m) médica (f) MÉ-JEE-KO (ah)

document documento DO-KO-MÉN-TO

dollar dólar DO-Lah-R

down abaixo, para baixo
ah-BO-SHoo / Pah-Rah BO-SHoo

downtown centro da cidade
SÉN-TRoo Dah SEE-Dah-JEE

drink (beverage) bebida BÉ-BEE-Dah

drugstore farmácia Fah-R-Mah-SEE-ah

dry cleaner tintureiro TEEN-Too-Rah-Roo

duck pato Pah-Too

E

ear orelha O-RÉL-Yah

ear drops gotas para o ouvido
GO-Tahs Pah-Rah oo O-VEE-Doo

early cedo SÉ-Doo

east leste LÉS-CHEE

easy fácil Fah-SEEL

eat (to) comer KO-MÉR

egg ovo O-Voo

egg (fried) ovo frito O-Voo FREE-Too

egg (scrambled) ovo mexido
O-Voo MÉ-SHEE-Doo

electricity eletricidade É-LÉ-TREE-SEE-Dah-JEE

elevator   elevador   ⓔ-Lⓔ-Vⓐ-DⓄʀ

embassy   embaixada   ⓔM-B①-SHⓐ-Dⓐ

emergency   emergência   ⓔ-Mⓔʀ-ZHⓔñg-Sⓔⓔ-ⓐ

England   Inglaterra   ⓔⓔñg-GLⓐ-Tⓔʀ-Hⓐ

English   inglês   ⓔⓔñg-GLⓔS

enough!   chega!   SHⓔ-Gⓐ

entrance   entrada   ⓔN-TRⓐ-Dⓐ

envelope   envelope   ⓔN-Vⓔ-LⓄ-Pⓔⓔ

evening   noite   Nⓞⓨ-CHⓔⓔ

everything   tudo   Tⓞⓞ-Dⓞⓞ

excellent   excelente   ⓔ-Sⓔ-Lⓔñg-CHⓔⓔ

excuse me   desculpe   JⓔS-KⓞⓞL-Pⓔⓔ

exit   saída   Sⓐ-ⓔⓔ-Dⓐ

expensive   caro (m) cara (f)   Kⓐ-Rⓞⓞ / Kⓐ-Rⓐ

eye   olho   ⓄL-Yⓞⓞ

eye drops   colírio   KⓄ-Lⓔⓔ-Rⓔⓔⓞⓞ

F

face   rosto   HⓄS-Tⓞⓞ

far   longe   LⓄñg-ZHⓔⓔ

fare   taxa, tarifa   Tⓐ-SHⓐ / Tⓐ-Rⓔⓔ-Fⓐ

fast   depressa   Jⓔⓔ-PRⓔ-Sⓐ

father   pai   P①

fax, fax machine fax FahX

February fevereiro Fē-Vē-RĀ-Roo

few pouco (m) pouca (f) PŌ-Koo / PŌ-Kah

few poucos (m,pl) poucas (f,pl)
  PŌ-KooS / PŌ-KahS

film (movie) filme FēL-Mē

finger dedo Dē-Doo

fire fogo FŌ-Goo

fire incêndio! ĪN-Sēñg-Jē-oo

first primeiro (m) primeira (f)
  PRē-MĀ-Roo / PRē-MĀ-Rah

fish peixe PĀ-SHē

flight vôo VŌ

florist shop floricultura FLO-Rē-KOL-Too-Rah

flower flor FLOR

food comida KO-Mē-Dah

foot pé Pē

fork garfo GahR-Foo

french fries batata frita Bah-Tah-Tah FRē-Tah

fresh fresco (m) fresca (f) FRēS-Koo / FRēS-Kah

Friday sexta-feira Sēs-Tah FĀ-Rah

fried frito (m) frita (f) FRē-Too / FRē-Tah

friend amigo (a) ah-Mē-Goo / ah-Mē-Gah

fruit   fruta   FR⊚⊚-T⍺ⓗ

funny   engraçado (m) engraçada (f)
   ⒠ñg-GR⍺ⓗ-S⍺ⓗ-D⊚⊚ / ⒠ñg-GR⍺ⓗ-S⍺ⓗ-D⍺ⓗ

G

gas station   posto de gasolina
   P⊙'S-T⊚⊚ J⒠⒠ G⍺S-⊙-L⒠⒠-N⍺ⓗ

gasoline   gasolina   G⍺S-⊙-L⒠⒠-N⍺ⓗ

gate   portão   P⊙R-T⊚ⓦñg

gentleman   senhor   S⒠ñg-Y⊙R

gift   presente   PR⒠-S⒠ñg-CH⒠⒠

girl   menina   M⒠-N⒠⒠-N⍺ⓗ

glass (drinking)   copo   K⊙'-P⊚⊚

glasses (eye)   óculos   ⊙'-K⊚⊚-L⊚⊚S

gloves   luvas   L⊚⊚'-V⍺ⓗS

go   ir   ⒠⒠R

gold   ouro   ⊙'-R⊚⊚

golf   golfe   G⊙L-F⒠⒠

golf course   campo de golfe
   K⍺ⓗñg-P⊚⊚ J⒠⒠ G⊙L-F⒠⒠

good   bom (m) boa (f)   B⊙ñg / B⊙'-⍺ⓗ

good-bye   até logo   ⍺ⓗ-T⒠' L⊙'-G⊚⊚

goose   ganso   G⍺ⓗ'N-S⊚⊚

grape   uva   ⊚⊚'-V⍺ⓗ

grateful agradecido (m) agradecida (f)
ah-GRah-Dē-SĒ-Doo / ah-GRah-Dē-SĒ-Dah

gray cinza SĒñg-Zah

green verde VĒR-JĒ

grocery store mercearia MĒR-SĒah-RĒ-ah

group grupo GRoo-Poo

guide guia GĒ-ah

H

hair cabelo Kah-BĒ-Loo

hairbrush escova de cabelo
ĒS-KŌ-Vah JĒ Kah-BĒ-Loo

haircut corte de cabelo
KŌR-CHĒ JĒ Kah-BĒ-Loo

ham presunto PRĒ-Sooñg-Too

hamburger hambúrguer HãM-Booß-GĒß

hand mão Mowñg

happy feliz FĒ-LĒS

have (to) ter TĒß

he ele Ē-LĒ

head cabeça Kah-BĒ-Sah

headache dor de cabeça DOß JĒ Kah-BĒ-Sah

health club (gym) academia ah-Kah-Dē-MĒ-ah

heart condition problema de coração
PßŌ-BLĒ-Mah JĒ KŌ-ßah-Sowñg

heart coração   KO-Rah-Sowñg

heat calor, aquecimento
   Kah-LOR / ah-KE-SEE-MEN-Too

hello oi   oy

help! (emergency) socorro!   SO-KO-Hoo

here aqui   ah-KEE

holiday feriado   FE-REE-ah-Doo

hospital hospital   OS-PEE-Tah L

hot dog cachorro quente   Kah-SHO-Hoo KEñg-CHEE

hotel hotel   O-TEL

hour hora   O-Rah

how como   KO-Moo

hurry up! depressa!   JEE-PREE-Sah

husband marido   Mah-REE-Doo

I

I eu   EOO

ice gelo   ZHE-Loo

ice cream sorvete   SOR-VE-CHEE

ice cubes cubos de gelo   KOO-BOOS JEE ZHE-LO

ill doente   DOO-EñG-CHEE

important importante   EEñg-POR-Tahñg-CHEE

indigestion indigestão   EEñg-JEE-JES-Towñg

information informação ⒠N-F⓪B-M⒜-S⓪Wñg

inn albergue ⒜L-B⒠B-G⒠⒠

interpreter intérprete ⒠ñg-T⓪B-PB⒠-CH⒠⒠

J

jacket paletó P⒜-L⒠⒠-T⓪

jam geléia ZH⒠-L⒜-⒜

January janeiro J⒜-N⒜-B⓪⓪

jewelry jóias ZH⓪Y-⒜S

jewelry store joalheria ZH⓪⒜-L⒠⒠-Y⒜-B⒠⒠-⒜

job emprego, trabalho
⒠ñg-PB⒠-G⓪⓪ / TB⒜-B⒜L-Y⓪⓪

juice suco S⓪⓪-K⓪⓪

July julho ZH⓪⓪L-Y⓪⓪

June junho ZH⓪⓪ñg-Y⓪⓪

K

ketchup ketchup, molho de tomate
K⒠-CH⓪-P⒠⒠ / M⓪L-Y⓪⓪ J⒠⒠ T⓪-M⒜-CH⒠⒠

key chave SH⒜-V⒠⒠

kiss posso te dar um beijo (literally: "May I kiss you.")
P⓪S-S⓪⓪ CH⒠⒠ D⒜B ⓪⓪ñg B⒜-J⓪⓪

knife faca F⒜-K⒜

know (to) saber S⒜-B⒠B

L

ladies room   banheiro feminino
  B@N-Y@́-R@@   F@́-M@@-N@@N-@@

lady   senhora   S@́ñg-YO-́R@

lamb   cordeiro   K@B-D@́-R@@

language   língua   L@́ñg-GW@

large   grande   GR@́ñg-J@@

late   tarde   T@R-J@@

laundry   lavanderia   L@-V@ñg-D@́-R@@-@

lawyer   advogado (m)   advogada (f)
  @-J@@-VO-G@-D@@ / @-J@@-VO-G@́-D@

left (direction)   esquerda   @S-K@B-D@

leg   perna   P@́B-N@

lemon   limão   L@@-M@́ñg

less   menos   M@́-N@@S

letter   carta   K@B-T@

lettuce   alface   @L-F@́-S@@

light   luz   L@@S

like (to)   gostar   G@S-T@B

lips   lábios   L@́-B@@-@@S

lipstick   batom   B@-T@ñg

little (amount)   pouco (m)   pouca (f)
  PO-́K@@ / PO-́K@

little (size) pequeno (m) pequena (f)
PĒ-KĒ-N⊚ / PĒ-KĒ-Nah

live (to) viver VĒ-VĒR

lobster lagosta Lah-GŌS-Tah

long longo (m) longa (f) LŌN-G⊚ / LŌN-Gah

lost perdido (m) perdida (f)
PĒR-JĒ-D⊚ / PĒR-JĒ-Dah

love amor ah-MŌR

luck sorte SŌR-CHĒ

luggage bagagem Bah-Gah-ZHĒñg

lunch almoço ahL-MŌ-S⊚

M

maid arrumadeira ah-H⊚-Mah-DĀ-Dah

maid (hotel) empregada ĒM-PRĒ-Gah-Dah

mail correio KŌ-HĀ-⊚

makeup maquiagem Mah-KĒah-ZHĒñg

man homem Ō-MĒñg

manager gerente ZHĒ-BĒñg-CHĒ

map mapa Mah-Pah

March março Mah-R-S⊚

market mercado MĒR-Kah-D⊚

matches (light) fósforos FŌS-F⊚-B⊚S

May maio MŌ-Y⊚

mayonnaise maionese MⒶ-YⓄ-NⒺ-ZⒺⒺ

meal refeição HⒺ-FⒺ-SⓄⓌñg

meat carne KⒶⒽB-NⒺⒺ

mechanic mecânico MⒺ-KⒶⒽ-NⒺⒺ-KⓄⓄ

meeting reunião HⒺ-ⓄⓄ-NⒺⒺ-ⓄⓌñg

mens' restroom banheiro masculino
    BⒶⒽN-YⒺ-BⓄⓄ MⒶⒽS-KⓄⓄ-LⒺⒺ-NⓄⓄ

menu cardápio KⒶⒽR-DⒶⒽ-PⒺⒺⓄ

message mensagem, recado
    MⒺN-SⒶⒽ-ZHⒺⒶñg / HⒺ-KⒶⒽ-DⓄⓄ

milk leite LⒶ-CHⒺⒺ

mineral water água mineral ⒶⒽ-GWⒶⒽ MⒺⒺ-NⒺ-BⓄⓌL

minute minuto MⒺⒺ-NⓄⓄ-TⓄⓄ

Miss Senhorita SⒺñg-YⓄ-BⒺⒺ-TⒶⒽ

mistake erro Ⓔ-HⓄⓄ

misunderstanding engano, malentendido
    ⒺⒺN-GⒶⒽ-NⓄⓄ / MⒶⒽL-ⒺN-TⒺN-JⒺⒺ-DⓄⓄ

moment momento MⓄ-MⒺN-TⓄⓄ

Monday segunda-feira SⒺⒺ-GⓄⓄñg-DⒶⒽ FⒶ-BⒶⒽ

money dinheiro DⒺⒺN-YⒶ-BⓄⓄ

month mês MⒺS

monument monumento MⓄ-NⓄⓄ-MⒺñg-TⓄⓄ

more mais MⒶS

morning manhã MⒶⒽñg-YⒶⒽñg

mosque mesquita MⒺS-KⒺⒺ-TⒶⒽ

mother mãe MOMng

mountain montanha MOMng-TahN-Yah

movies cinema SEE-NA-Mah

Mr. Senhor SEMng-OB

Mrs. Senhora SEMng-O-Bah

much (too) muito MWEEng-Too

museum museu MOO-ZA-oo

mushrooms cogumelos KO-GOO-ME-LOOS

music música MOO-ZEE-Kah

mustard mostarda MOS-TahR-DO

N

nail polish esmalte para unhas
ES-MahL-CHEE PAh-Rah OON-EE-YahS

name nome NO-MEE

napkin guardanapo GWahB-Dah-Nah-Poo

napkin (sanitary) módess MO-DES

near perto PEB-Too

neck nuca NOO-Kah

need (to) preciso / necessito
PBEE-SEE-Zoo / NES-SEE-SEE-Too

never nunca NOOng-Kah

newspaper jornal ZHOB-NowL

news stand banca de jornal
Bahng-Kah JEE ZHOB-NowL

next time   próxima vez   PRO-SEE-Mah VeS

night   noite   Noy-CHEE

nightclub   boate   BO-ah-CHEE

no   não   Nowñg

no smoking   não fumar   Nowñg Foo-MahB

noon   meio-dia   MA-oo DEE-ah

north   norte   NOB-CHEE

notary   notário (m) notária (f)
   NO-Tah'B-EEoo / NO-Tah'B-EEah

November   novembro   NO-VeM-BRoo

now   agora   ah-GO-Bah

number   número   Noo-Me-Boo

nurse   enfermeiro (m) enfermeira (f)
   EEñg-FeB-MA-Boo / EEñg-FeB-MA-Bah

O

occupied   ocupado (m) ocupada (f)
   O-Koo-Pah-Doo / O-Koo-Pah-Dah

ocean   oceano   O-Seah-Noo

October   outubro   O-Too-BRoo

officer   oficial   O-FEE-SEE-ahL

oil   óleo   OL-Yoo

omelet   omelete   O-Me-Le-CHEE

one-way (traffic)   sentido único
   SeN-CHEE-Doo oo-NEE-Koo

onion cebola Sẽ-BŌ-Lah

open (to) abrir ah-BRẼR

opera ópera Ó-Pẽ-Rah

operator telefonista
Tẽ-Lẽ-FŌ-NẼ-STah

optician um oculista (m) uma oculista (f)
ooñg Ō-Koo-LẼS-Tah / oo-Mah Ō-Koo-LẼS-Tah

orange (color) laranja Lah-Rahñg-ZHah

orange (fruit) laranja Lah-Rahñg-ZHah

order (to) pedido Pẽ-Jẽ-Doo

original original Ō-Rẽ-ZHẼ-Nõwl

owner proprietário (m) proprietária (f)
PRŌ-PRẼẼ-Tah́R-Ẽoo / PRŌ-PRẼẼ-Tah́R-Ẽah

oysters ostras ÓS-TRahS

P

package pacote Pah-KŌ-CHẼ

paid pago Pah-Goo

pain dor DŌR

painting pintura Pẽñg-Too-Rah

paper papel Pah-PẽL

parking lot estacionamento
ẽS-Tah-SẼŌ-Nah-MẼN-Too

partner (business) sócio (m) sócia (f)
SÓ-SẼ-oo / SÓ-SẼ-Yah

party festa F(ẽ)S-T(ah)

passenger passageiro (m) passageira (f)
P(ah)-S(ah)-ZH(A)-B(oo) / P(ah)-S(ah)-ZH(A)-B(ah)

passport passaporte P(ah)-S(ah)-P(O)B-CH(ee)

pasta massas M(ah)-S(ah)

pastry massa folhada M(ah)-S(ah) F(O)L-Y(ah)-D(ah)

pen caneta K(ah)-N(ẽ)-T(ah)

pencil lápis L(ah)-P(ee)S

pepper pimenta P(ee)-M(ẽ)ñg-T(ah)

perfume perfume P(ẽ)B-F(oo)-M(ee)

person pessoa P(ẽ)-S(O)-(ah)

pharmacist farmacêutico (m) farmacêutica (f)
F(ah)B-M(ah)-S(ẽ)(oo)-CH(ee)-K(oo) / F(ah)B-M(ah)-S(ẽ)(oo)-CH(ee)-K(ah)

pharmacy farmácia F(ah)B-M(ah)-S(ee)(ah)

phone book lista telefônica
L(ee)S-T(ah) T(ẽ)-L(ẽ)-F(O)-N(ee)-K(ah)

photo foto, fotografia F(O)-T(oo) / F(O)-T(O)-GB(ah)-F(ee)-(ah)

photographer fotógrafo (m) fotógrafa (f)
F(O)-T(O)-GB(ah)-F(oo) / F(O)-T(O)-GB(ah)-F(ah)

pillow travesseiro TB(ah)-V(ẽ)-S(A)-B(oo)

pink rosa H(O)-Z(ah)

plastic plástico PL(ah)S-CH(ee)-K(oo)

plate prato PB(ah)-T(oo)

please por favor P(O)B F(ah)-V(O)B

pleasure   prazer   PRah-ZēR

police   polícia   PO-Lēē-Sēē-ah

police station   delegacia de polícia
Dēē-Lē-Gah-Sēē-ah   Jēē   PO-Lēē-Sēē-ah

pork   porco   POB-Koo

porter   carregador   Kah-Hē-Gah-DOB

post office   agência de correio
ah-ZHēN-Sēē-ah   Jēē   KO-Hā-oo

postcard   cartão postal   Kah-B-Towñg   POS-Towl

potato   batata   Bah-Tah-Tah

pregnant   grávida   GRah-Vēē-Dah

prescription   receita   Hē-Sā-Tah

price   preço   PRē-Soo

problem   problema   PRO-BLē-Mah

profession   profissão   PRO-Fēē-Sowñg

public   público (m)   pública (f)
Poo-BLēē-Koo / Poo-BLēē-Kah

public telephone   telefone público
Tē-Lē-FO-Nēē   Poo-BLēē-Koo

purified   purificado (m)   purificada (f)
Poo-Bēē-Fēē-Kah-Doo / Poo-Bēē-Fēē-Kah-Dah

purple   roxo (m)   roxa (f)   HO-SHoo / HO-SHah

purse   bolsa   BOL-Sah

Q

quality   qualidade   KWah-LEE-Dah-JEE

question   pergunta   PER-Goong-Tah

quickly   rápido   Hah-PEE-Doo

quickly   rapidamente   Hah-PEE-Dah-MEng-CHEE

quiet   quieto (m) quieta (f)   KEEE-Too / KEEE-Tah

quiet!   silêncio!   SEE-LEN-SEEoo

R

radio   rádio   Hah-Joo

railroad   estrada de ferro   EES-TRah-Dah JEE FE-Hoo

rain   chuva   SHoo-Vah

raincoat   capa de chuva   Kah-Pah JEE SHoo-Vah

ramp   rampa   HahM-Pah

rare (cooked)   mal passado (m) mal passada (f)
MahL Pah S-Sah-Doo / MahL Pah S-Sah-Dah

razor blades   lâminas de barbear
Lah-MEE-NahS JEE Bah B-BEE-ah B

ready   pronto (m) pronta (f)
PROng-Too / PROng-Tah

receipt   recibo   HE-SEE-Boo

recommend (to)   recomendar   RE-KO-MEN-Dah B

red   vermelho (m) vermelha (f)
VE B-MEL-Yoo / VE B-MEL-Yah

repeat! repita! HĒ-PĒ-Tah

reservation reserva HĒ-SĒB-Vah

restaurant restaurante HĒS-Tow-Bāñg-CHĒ

return retornar, voltar HĒ-TOB-Nah'B / VOL-Tah'B

rice arroz ah-HŌS

rich rico (m) rica (f) BĒ-Koo / BĒ-Kah

right (correct) correto (m) correta (f)
    KO-HĒ-Too / KO-HĒ-Tah

right (direction) direita JĒ-BĀ-Tah

road estrada ĒS-TBah-Dah

room quarto KWah'B-Too

round trip ida-e-volta ĒE-DĀ ĒE VŌL-Tah

S

safe (hotel) cofre KŌ-FBĒ

salad salada Sah-Lah-Dah

sale venda VĒN-Dah

salmon salmão Sah-L-Mowñg

salt sal SahL

sandwich sanduíche Sah-N-Doo-WĒ-SHĒ

Saturday sábado Sah-Bah-Doo

scissors tesoura TĒ-ZŌ-Bah

sculpture escultura ĒS-Kool-Too-Bah

seafood frutos do mar FBoo-ToS Doo Mah'B

season estação ⒠S-T⒜-S⒪ⓦñg

seat assento ⒜-S⒠ñg-T⒪⒪

secretary secretário (m) secretária (f)
S⒠-KR⒠-T⒜-REE-⒪⒪ / S⒠-KR⒠-T⒜-REE-⒜

section seção S⒠-S⒪ⓦñg

September setembro S⒠-T⒠ñg-BR⒪⒪

service serviço S⒠R-V⒠-S⒪⒪

several diversos (m) diversas (f)
vários (m) várias (f)

J⒠-V⒠R-S⒪⒪S / J⒠-V⒠R-S⒜S

V⒜R-⒠⒠⒪⒪S / V⒜R-⒠⒠⒜S

shampoo xampu SH⒜ñg-P⒪⒪

sheets (bed) lençól (sg) lençóis (pl)
L⒠N-S⒪L / L⒠N-S⒪ⓥS

shirt camisa K⒜-M⒠⒠-Z⒜

shoe sapato S⒜-P⒜-T⒪⒪

shoe store loja de sapatos
L⒪-ZH⒜ J⒠ S⒜-P⒜-T⒪⒪S

shopping center centro comercial
S⒠ñg-TR⒪⒪ K⒪-M⒠R-S⒠-⒜L

shower chuveiro SH⒪⒪-VⒶ-R⒪⒪

shrimp camarão K⒜-M⒜-B⒪ⓦñg

sick doente D⒪-⒠ñg-CH⒠

sign (display) mostra / sinal M⒪S-TR⒜ / S⒠-N⒪ⓥL

signature assinatura ⒜-S⒠N-⒜-T⒪⒪-R⒜

silence! silêncio! SEE-LEN-SEE-oo

single (unmarried) solteiro (m) solteira (f)
SOL-TA-Boo / SOL-TA-Bah

single único (m) única (f)
ooN-EE-Koo / ooN-EE-Kah

sir senhor SEñg-YOB

sister irmã EB-Mahñg

size tamanho Tah-Mahñg-Yoo

skin pele PE-LEE

skirt saia Sah-Yah

sleeve manga MahN-Gah

slowly lentamente LEN-Tah-MEñg-CHEE

small pequeno (m) pequena (f)
PE-KE-N-oo / PE-KE-Nah

smile (to) sorriso SO-HEE-Zoo

smoke (to) fumar Foo-MahB

soap sabão, sabonete Sah-Bow / Sah-BO-NE-CHEE

socks meias MA-ahS

some alguns (m,pl) algumas (f,pl)
ahL-GooNS / ahL-Goo-MahS

something algo ahL-Goo

sometimes às vezes ahZ VE-ZEES

soon logo LO-Goo

sorry desculpe JES-KooL-PEE

soup   sopa   SŌ-P@h

south   sul   S@L

souvenir   lembrança   L@M-BR@ñg-S@h

Spanish   espanhol   @S-P@N-YŌL

speciality   especialidade   @S-P@-S@@h-L@@-D@h-J@@

speed   velocidade   V@-L@-S@@-D@h-J@@

spoon   colher   K@L-Y@R

sport   esporte   @S-P@R-CH@@

spring (season)   primavera   PR@@-M@h-V@-R@h

stairs   escada   @S-K@h-D@h

stamp   selo   S@-L@

station   estação   @S-T@h-S@ñg

steak   bife   B@@-F@@

steamed   cozido a vapor
    K@-Z@@-D@@   @h   V@h-P@R

stop!   pare!   P@h-R@@

store   loja   L@-ZH@h

storm   tempestade   T@M-P@S-T@h-J@@

straight ahead   em frente   @@ñg-FR@ñg-CH@@

strawberry   morango   M@-R@h-N-G@@

street   rua   H@@-@h

string   barbante   B@R-B@hñg-CH@@

subway   metrô   M@-TR@

sugar açúcar ⓐ-Sⓞⓞ-KⓐⓑR

suit (clothes) terno TⓔⓑR-Nⓞⓞ

suitcase mala Mⓐⓑ-Lⓐⓑ

Summer verão VⓔⓑR-ⓞⓦñg

sun sol SⓞL

suntan lotion bronzeador BRⓞN-Zⓔⓔ-ⓐⓑ-DⓞⓑR

Sunday domingo Dⓞ-Mⓔⓔñg-Gⓞⓞ

sunglasses óculos de sol Ⓞ-Kⓞⓞ-LⓞⓞS Jⓔⓔ SⓞL

supermarket supermercado
Sⓞⓞ-PⓔⓑR-MⓔⓑR-Kⓐⓑ-Dⓞⓞ

surprise surpresa SⓞⓞR-PRⓔⓑ-Zⓐⓑ

sweet doce Dⓞⓑ-Sⓔⓔ

swim (to) nadar Nⓐⓑ-DⓐⓑR

swimming pool piscina Pⓔⓔ-Sⓔⓔ-Nⓐⓑ

synagogue sinagoga Sⓔⓔ-Nⓐⓑ-Gⓞⓑ-Gⓐⓑ

table mesa Mⓔⓑ-Zⓐⓑ

tampon tampão Tⓐⓑñg-Pⓞⓦñg

tape (sticky) durex Dⓞⓞ-RⓔⓑKS

tape recorder gravador GRⓐⓑ-Vⓐⓑ-DⓞⓑR

tax imposto ⓔⓔñg-PⓞⓑS-Tⓞⓞ

taxi táxi TⓐⓑK-Sⓔⓔ

tea chá SHⓐⓑ

telephone   telefone   TĒ-LĒ-FŌ-NĒE

television   televisão   TĒ-LĒ-VĒE-ZŌŵñg

temperature   temperatura   TĒñg-PĒ-BĒah-TŌŌ-BĒah

temple   templo   TĒM-PLŌŌ

tennis   tênis   TĒ-NĒES

tennis court   quadra de tênis
KWĕah-DBĕah   JĒE   TĒ-NĒES

thank you!   obrigado! (m)   obrigada! (f)
Ō-BRĒE-Gĕah-DŌŌ   /   Ō-BRĒE-Gĕah-Dĕah

that   aquele (m)   aquela (f)   aquilo
ĕah-KĒ-LĒE   /   ĕah-KĒ-Lĕah   /   ĕah-KĒE-LŌŌ

the   o (m,s)   a (f,s)   os (m,pl)   as (f,pl)
ŌŌ   /   ĕah   /   ŌŌS   /   ĕahS

theater (movie)   cinema   SĒE-NĀ-Mĕah

there   lá   Lĕah

they   eles (m)   elas (f)   ĒLĒES   /   ĒLĕahS

this   este (m) / esta (f) / isto (thing)
ĒS-CHĒE   /   ĒS-Tĕah   /   ĒES-TŌŌ

thread   fio, linha   FĒE-ŌŌ   /   LĒEñg-Yĕah

throat   garganta   GĕahB-Gĕahñg-Tĕah

Thursday   quinta-feira   KĒEN-Tĕah   FĀ-BĕAh

ticket   bilhete, passagem
BĒEL-YĒ-CHĒE   /   Pĕah-Sĕah-ZHĀñg

tie   gravata   GBĕah-Vĕah-Tĕah

time tempo TĔñg-Poo

tip (gratuity) gorjeta GOR-ZHĔ-Tah

tire pneu PĔ-NÁ-oo

tired cansado (m) cansada (f)
Kahñg-Sah-Doo / Kahñg-Sah-Dah

toast (bread) torrada TO-Hah-Dah

tobacco tabaco Tah-Bah-Koo

today hoje Ó-ZHee

toe dedo do pé DĔ-Doo Doo Pĕ

together junto ZHooñg-Too

toilet toalete TOah-LĔ-CHee

toilet paper papel higiênico
Pah-PĔL ee-ZHee-ĕ-Nee-Koo

tomato tomate TO-Mah-CHee

tomorrow amanhã ah-Mahñg-Yahñg

toothache dor de dente DOR Jee DĔñg-CHee

toothbrush escova de dentes
ĕS-KÓ-Vah Jee DĔñg-CHeeS

toothpaste pasta de dentes Pah S-Tah Jee DĔñg-CHeeS

toothpick palito Pah-LEE-Too

tour excursão ĕS-Koo B-Sowñg

tourist turista Too-BeeS-Tah

tourist office agência de turismo
Á-ZHÁñg-See-ah Jee Too-BeeS-Moo

towel toalha   TO-ahL-Yah

train trem   TRAñg

travel agency agência de viagem
 ah-ZHEñg-SEE-ah JEE VEE-ah-ZHEñg

traveler's check cheque de viagem
 SHEE-KEE JEE VEE-ah-ZHEñg

trip viagem   VEE-ah-ZHEE

trousers calças   KahL-SahS

trout truta   TRoo-Tah

truth verdade   VER-Dah-JEE

Tuesday terça-feira   TER-Sah FA-Rah

turkey peru   PEE-Roo

U

umbrella guarda-chuva   GWahB-Dah SHoo-Vah

understand (to) compreender, entender
 KOñg-PREE-eñg-DER / eN-Teñg-DER

underwear roupa de baixo   HO-Pah JEE BI-SHoo

United Kingdom Reino Unido   HA-Noo oo-NEE-Doo

United States Estados Unidos
 EES-Tah-DooS oo-NEE-DooS

university universidade   oo-NEE-VER-SEE-Dah-JEE

up para cima, encima
 Pah-Rah SEE-Mah / eN-SEE-Mah

urgent urgente   oo-ZHEñg-CHEE

V

vacant desocupado (m) desocupada (f)
JĚ-SŌ-KOO-PAH-DOO / JĚ-SŌ-KOO-PAH-DAH

vacation férias FĚ-REE-AHS

valuable valioso (m) valiosa (f)
VÃ-LEE-Ó-ZOO / VÃ-LEE-Ó-ZAH

value valor VAH-LÕR

vanilla baunilha BOW-NEEL-YAH

veal vitela VEE-TĚL-AH

vegetables verduras VĚR-DOOR-AHS

view vista VEES-TAH

vinegar vinagre VEE-NAH-GREE

voyage viagem VEE-AH-ZHĚñg

W

wait! espere! EES-PĚ-REE

waiter / waitress garçom / garçonete
GAHR-SŌñg / GAHR-SŌ-NĚ-CHEE

want (to) querer KĚ-RĚR

wash (to) lavar LAH-VAHR

watch out! cuidado! KWEE-DAH-DOO

water água AH-GWAH

watermelon melancia MĚ-LAHñg-SEE-AH

we nós NAHS

weather tempo Tĕñg-P🔘

Wednesday quarta-feira KW🔘B-T🔘h F🅐-B🔘h

week semana Sĕ-M🔘h-N🔘h

weekend fim de semana Fĕĕñg Jĕĕ Sĕ-M🔘h-N🔘h

welcome bem-vindo (m) bem-vinda (f)
   B🅐ñg Vĕĕñg-D🔘 / B🅐ñg Vĕĕñg-D🔘h

well done (cooked) bem passado (m) bem passada(f)
   B🅐ñg P🔘S-S🔘h-D🔘 / B🅐ñg P🔘S-S🔘h-D🔘h

west oeste 🔘-ĕS-CHĕĕ

wheelchair cadeira de rodas
   K🔘h-D🅐'-B🔘h Jĕĕ H🔘-D🔘hS

when? quando? KW🔘hñg-D🔘

where? onde? 🔘ñg-Jĕĕ

which? qual? KW🔘L

white branco (m) branca (f) BB🔘hñg-K🔘 / BB🔘hñg-K🔘h

who? quem? K🅐ñg

why? porquê? P🔘B-Kĕ

wife esposa, mulher ĕĕS-P🔘-Z🔘h / M🔘L-Yĕ'B

wind vento Vĕñg-T🔘

window janela ZH🔘h-Nĕ'-L🔘h

wine list carta de vinhos K🔘hB-T🔘h Jĕĕ VĕĕN-Y🔘S

wine vinho Vĕĕñg-Y🔘

Winter inverno ĕĕñg-Vĕ'B-N🔘

with com KOñg

woman mulher MooL-YëR

wonderful maravilhoso (m) maravilhosa (f)
Mah-Rah-VEEL-YO-Zoo / Mah-Rah-VEEL-YO-Zah

world mundo Mooñg-Doo

wrong errado (m) errada (f) ë-Hah-Doo / ë-Hah-Dah

XYZ

year ano ah-Noo

yellow amarelo (m) amarela (f)
ah-Mah-Rë-Loo / ah-Mah-Rë-Lah

yes sim Sëñg

yesterday ontem Oñg-Tañg

you você (s), vocês (pl) VO-Sâ / VO-SâS

zipper zíper Zëë-PëR

zoo jardím zoológico Jah-Jëñg ZO-LO-ZHëë-Koo

THANKS!

The nicest thing you can say to anyone in any language is "Thank you." Try some of these languages using the incredible Vowel Symbol System.

Spanish	French
GRah'-SEE-ahS	MĕR-SEE

German	Italian
Dah'N-Kuh	GRah'T-SEE-ĕ

Japanese	Chinese
DO-MO	SHEEĕ SHEEĕ

Swedish	Portuguese
TⓐK	Ⓞ-BRⒺⒺ-Gⓐ́-DⓄⓄ

Arabic	Greek
SHⓄⓄ-KRⓐN	ⓔ̃F-Hⓐ-RⒺⒺ-STⓄ́

Hebrew	Russian
TⓄ-Dⓐ́	SPⓐ-SⒺⒺ́-Bⓐ

Swahili	Dutch
ⓐ-Sⓐ́N-TⒶ	Dⓐ́NK ⓄⓄ

Tagalog	Hawaiian
Sⓐ-Lⓐ-Mⓐ́T	Mⓐ-Hⓐ́-LⓄ

INDEX